Great Meals in Minutes was created by Rebus, Inc. and published by Time-Life Books.

Rebus, Inc.

Publisher: Rodney Friedman
Editorial Director: Shirley Tomkievicz

Editor: Marya Dalrymple
Art Director: Ronald Gross
Managing Editor: Brenda Goldberg
Senior Editor: Charles Blackwell
Food Editor and Food Stylist: Grace Young
Photographer: Steven Mays
Prop Stylist: Cathryn Schwing
Staff Writer: Alexandra Greeley
Assistant Editor: Bonnie J. Slotnick
Editorial Assistant: Ned Miller
Assistant Food Stylist: Karen Hatt
Photography Assistant: Edward Santalone
Recipe Tester: Gina Palombi Barclay
Production Assistant: Lorna Bieber

For information about any Time-Life book, please write:
Reader Information
Time-Life Books
541 North Fairbanks Court
Chicago, Illinois 60611

Library of Congress Cataloging in Publication Data
Late-night supper menus.
  (Great meals in minutes)
  Includes index.
  1. Suppers. 2. Menus. 3. Cooks—United States—
Biography. I. Time-Life Books. II. Series.
TX738.L37 1985   641.5′4   85-1087
ISBN 0-86706-286-X (lib. bdg.)
ISBN 0-86706-285-1 (retail ed.)

Time-Life Books Inc.
is a wholly owned subsidiary of

Time Incorporated

Founder: Henry R. Luce 1898–1967
Editor-in-Chief: Henry Anatole Grunwald
President: J. Richard Munro
Chairman of the Board: Ralph P. Davidson
Corporate Editor: Jason McManus
Group Vice President, Books: Reginald K. Brack Jr.
Vice President, Books: George Artandi

Time-Life Books Inc.

Editor: George Constable
Executive Editor: George Daniels
Editorial General Manager: Neal Goff
Director of Design: Louis Klein
Editorial Board: Dale M. Brown, Roberta Conlan, Ellen Phillips, Gerry Schremp, Gerald Simons, Rosalind Stubenberg, Kit van Tulleken, Henry Woodhead
Director of Research: Phyllis K. Wise
Director of Photography: John Conrad Weiser

President: William J. Henry
Senior Vice President: Christopher T. Linen
Vice Presidents: Stephen L. Bair, Robert A. Ellis, John M. Fahey Jr., Juanita T. James, James L. Mercer, Joanne A. Pello, Paul R. Stewart, Christian Strasser

Editorial Operations
Design: Ellen Robling (assistant director)
Copy Room: Diane Ullius
Editorial Operations: Caroline A. Boubin (manager)
Production: Celia Beattie
Quality Control: James J. Cox (director), Sally Collins
Library: Louise D. Forstall

SERIES CONSULTANT
Margaret E. Happel is the author of *Ladies' Home Journal Adventures in Cooking, Ladies' Home Journal Handbook of Holiday Cuisine,* and other best-selling cookbooks, as well as the translator and adapter of Rebecca Hsu Hiu Min's *Delights of Chinese Cooking.* A food consultant based in New York City, she has been director of the food department of *Good Housekeeping* and editor of *American Home* magazine.

WINE CONSULTANT
Tom Maresca combines a full-time career teaching English literature with writing about and consuming fine wines. He is the author of *Mastering Wine a Taste at a Time.*

Cover: Warren Mah's pork and scallion rolls, stir-fried carrots, snow peas, and *enoki* mushrooms, and steamed white rice. See pages 76–77.

Great Meals
IN MINUTES

LATE-NIGHT
SUPPER
MENUS

TIME-LIFE BOOKS, ALEXANDRIA, VIRGINIA

Contents

Meet the Cooks

VICTORIA FAHEY

Born in the Midwest, Victoria Fahey now lives in California, where she is the chef for Curds & Whey, an Oakland specialty food store, charcuterie, and catering business. She also develops new products for The New Oakland Food Company, a wholesaler of specialty foods.

EVELYNE SLOMON

Evelyne Slomon is a self-taught cook who learned the art of cuisine from family and friends in France. She operates her own cooking school in Manhattan, specializing in French cooking and pizza workshops, and she is the author of *The Pizza Book: Everything There Is to Know About the World's Greatest Pie*. She is now at work on a country French cookbook.

MARY CLEAVER

After training in restaurant kitchens, Mary Cleaver worked as executive chef for a large corporation in New York City. She now owns and operates the Cleaver Company, a Manhattan catering firm, and teaches cooking at the New School for Social Research in Manhattan and at Kings Cooking Studio in Caldwell, New Jersey. She is a member of the New York Women's Culinary Alliance.

SARAH BELK RIAN

Sarah Belk Rian studied cooking at L'Ecole de Cuisine La Varenne in Paris. She has worked as associate food and wine editor of *House & Garden* magazine and as a freelance food writer, contributing to numerous national publications. She is food and entertainment editor of *House Beautiful* and is working on a cookbook featuring updated classic recipes from the southeastern United States.

DAVID KIMMEL AND STEVEN PETUSEVSKY

David Kimmel and his colleague Steven Petusevsky are both graduates of the Culinary Institute of America. David Kimmel has taught restaurant design at the institute and is a member of its board of trustees. Steven Petusevsky has been employed by several hotels, among them the Woodstock Inn and the Frankfurt Inter-Continental. Since 1982 they have worked together at Caraway Associates, a New York-based food-consulting company.

JANE MORIMOTO AND ALICE GAUTSCH

Both home economists, Jane Morimoto and Alice Gautsch are currently test kitchen supervisor and senior vice president/director, respectively, for Seattle-based Pacific Kitchens, which specializes in consumer food public relations. Jane Morimoto has also worked for the USDA, Lawry's Foods, and the *Seattle Times*. Alice Gautsch was on the food staff of *McCall's* magazine and has worked for two major food companies.

WARREN MAH

A native of Portland, Oregon, Warren Mah trained as a cook in his family's Chinese restaurants. Since 1978, he has worked as a chef-instructor in Oriental cooking at the Culinary Institute of America in Hyde Park, New York. He also travels nationwide for the institute, teaching classes in baking and basic and advanced cooking, and gives seminars for the National Restaurant Association.

CHARLOTTE TURGEON

A professional cookbook editor and author, and a graduate of the Cordon Bleu, Charlotte Turgeon was an editor of *Larousse Gastronomique*. She has written *The All-American Cookbook*, *The Fiber and Bran Better Health Cookbook*, and the *Encyclopedia of Creative Cooking*. She currently runs her own cooking school in Amherst, Massachusetts.

MARGARET FRASER

Home economist Margaret Fraser lives in Toronto, Canada, where she manages her own consulting business, specializing in food styling for magazines, television commercials, and product packaging. She is also associate food editor at *Canadian Living*.

Late-night Supper Menus in Minutes
GREAT MEALS FOR FOUR IN AN HOUR OR LESS

A late-night supper can be a posh sit-down dinner, a casual buffet, or simply a quick light meal prepared with friends. Whether enjoyed in the dining room or the kitchen, in the backyard or on a boat, this meal should convey a convivial, leisurely mood.

Pretexts for a late-night supper are not difficult to find. You may want to extend an evening's entertainment and companionship by inviting people home after a play, a sports event, or some other outing. You might celebrate a special occasion such as New Year's Eve, a birthday, or an anniversary. Or cap off an evening of home movies, cards, or board games.

A late-night supper can begin anytime and go on until midnight, or even until dawn. To make your party successful, organize it as carefully as you would any other, right down to the last folded napkin. Have the table, sideboard, or trays set, and all kitchen equipment ready early in the day. Chill beverages, if necessary. Because of the late hour, guests may be very hungry: Whenever possible, have all foods ready to cook, or precook and refrigerate dishes in advance for instant serving or reheating when the time comes.

Planning your menu is easy because a late-night supper can be as basic as baked eggs or as elegant as a soufflé roll with Calvados cream. Most beverages are appropriate, too: Champagne, *sake*, warm milk laced with brandy, herbal teas, mineral water sparked with lemon or lime juice, and regular or decaffeinated coffees are just a few possibilities.

On the following pages, eleven of America's most talented cooks present 27 complete menus featuring ideas for late-night suppers, from individual mini-pizzas to an elegant golden caviar pie served with an unusual frittata of leeks and peaches. There are also recipes for Mexican, country French, American regional, Canadian, and Japanese-inspired dishes, many of which can be served either hot or cold and may be prepared well in advance of serving. A number of these dishes also work well as lunches or brunches.

Each menu, which serves four people, can be prepared in an hour or less, and the cooks focus on a new kind of American cuisine that borrows ideas and techniques from around the world but also values our native traditions. They use fresh produce, with no powdered sauces or other dubious shortcuts. The other ingredients called for (vinegars, spices, herbs, and so on) are all of very high quality and are usually available in supermarkets or specialty food stores.

The cooks and the kitchen staff have meticulously planned and tested the menus for appearance as well as for taste, as the accompanying photographs show: The vegetables are brilliant and fresh, the visual combinations appetizing. The table settings feature bright colors, simple flower arrangements, and attractive but not necessarily expensive serving dishes.

For each menu, the Editors, with advice from the cooks, suggest wines and other beverages. And there are suggestions for the use of leftovers and for complementary dishes and desserts. On each menu page, you will find a number of other tips, from an easy method for stuffing quahogs to advice for selecting fresh produce.

BEFORE YOU START
Great Meals in Minutes is designed for efficiency and ease. This book will work best for you if you follow these suggestions:

1. Refresh your memory with the few simple cooking techniques on the following pages. They will quickly become second nature, and you will produce professional-quality meals in minutes.

2. Read the menus before you shop. Each lists the ingredients you will need, in the order that you would expect to shop for them. Many items will already be on your pantry shelf.

3. Check the equipment list on page 14. Good sharp knives and pots and pans of the right shape and material are essential for making great meals in minutes. This may be the time to buy a few things: The right equipment can turn cooking from a necessity into a creative experience.

4. Set out everything you need before you start to cook. The lists at the beginning of each menu tell just what is required. To save effort, always keep your ingredients in the same place so you can reach for them instinctively.

5. Follow the start-to-finish steps for each menu. That way, you can be sure of having the entire meal ready to serve in an hour.

SETTING THE MOOD
Because late-night suppers are uncomplicated meals, you will have the time to indulge in some of the frills of enter-

Glowing candles in a sterling candelabra, iced champagne, fine china, and a beautiful appetizer of caviar and egg canapés set an elegant tone for a late-night gathering.

Cooking at high temperatures will be less dangerous if you follow a few simple tips:

▶ Water added to hot fat will always cause spattering. If possible, pat foods dry with a cloth or paper towel before you add them to the hot oil.

▶ Place food gently into any pan containing hot fat, or the fat will spatter.

▶ If you are boiling or steaming some foods while sautéing others, place the pots on the stove top far enough apart so that the water is unlikely to splash into the hot fat.

▶ Turn pot handles inward, so that you do not accidentally knock over a pot containing hot foods or liquids.

▶ Remember that alcohol—wine, brandy, or spirits—may catch fire when you add it to a very hot pan. If this happens, step back for your own protection and quickly cover the pan with a lid. The fire will instantly subside, and the food will not be spoiled.

▶ Keep pot holders and mitts close enough to be handy while cooking, but *never* hang them over the burners or lay them on the stove top.

---

taining to dress up your party. Creating interesting table settings with fanciful flower arrangements and employing imaginative candlelighting are some of the ways to set a special tone for the evening.

Making Stock

Although canned chicken broth or stock is all right for emergencies, homemade chicken stock has a rich flavor that is hard to match. Moreover, the commercial broths—particularly the canned ones—are likely to be oversalted.

To make your own stock, save chicken parts as they accumulate and put them in a bag in the freezer; then have a rainy-day stock-making session, using the recipe below. The skin from a yellow onion will add color; the optional veal bone will add extra flavor and richness to the stock.

Basic Chicken Stock

3 pounds bony chicken parts, such as wings,
    back, and neck
1 veal knuckle (optional)
3 quarts cold water
1 yellow unpeeled onion, stuck with 2 cloves
2 stalks celery with leaves, cut in two
12 crushed peppercorns
2 carrots, scraped and cut into 2-inch lengths
4 sprigs parsley
1 bay leaf
1 tablespoon fresh thyme, or 1 teaspoon dried
Salt (optional)

1. Wash chicken parts and veal knuckle (if you are using it) thoroughly under cold running water. Place in large soup kettle or stockpot (any big pot) with the remaining ingredients—except salt. Cover pot and bring to a boil over medium heat.
2. Lower heat and simmer stock, partly covered, 2 to 3 hours. Skim foam and scum from top of stock several times. Add salt to taste after stock has cooked 1 hour.
3. Strain stock through fine sieve placed over large bowl. Discard solids. Let stock cool uncovered (this will speed cooling process). When completely cool, refrigerate. Fat will rise and congeal conveniently at top. You may skim it off and discard it or leave it as a protective covering.

Yield: About 10 cups

When planning your gathering, first decide whether you want a casual eat-where-you-please meal or a more formal sit-down dinner. Then determine the menu. Check to see if you have linens, plates, serving pieces and trays, vases and candleholders that suit the occasion and complement the food. You do not need an extensive or costly inventory for a late-night supper; for this kind of entertaining, you can carefully mix and match textures and colors of your tableware, and even pair fine sterling with casual pottery.

Placemats and tablecloths set the stage. When selecting placemats, be imaginative: Use fabric, straw, or wooden mats in rectangles, rounds, or free-form shapes. Or cover your table completely with a full-sized cloth—a quilt, a floral-printed sheet, or a batik dress length. Dark colors convey a restful, perhaps romantic mood, especially in conjunction with candlelight. If you plan a portable meal, you can cover trays with placemats, or if the trays are attractive, forego linens altogether.

Flowers

Freshly cut flowers are always a dramatic centerpiece, particularly if you select an unusual vase or other container, such as a soup tureen, wide-mouth bottle, compote, earthenware jug, basket, or decorative ceramic or silver vessel. Whatever flowers and holder you use, arrange the floral centerpiece so it does not obstruct vision and disrupt conversation: Flowers should be at eye level or lower. Sit down while you arrange the flowers so you get the proper perspective. For a formal late-night supper, you can set out tiny vases at each guest's place; for a mobile meal, place a small vase or a single stem on each tray.

Candles

Soft lighting at night promotes intimacy and ambience and is restful on the eyes. Guests will appreciate this gesture as long as they can see what they are eating.

Candles are a good way to produce subtle lighting. If your dining room or entertaining area does not lend itself to using only candles, supplement them with dimmed lamp light. At a small table, group a few low candles in place of a centerpiece, or if the table is crowded, place candles single-file down the center of the table. Alternatively, cluster several short candles at either end of the table, or put one at each guest's place. If serving on trays, you may want to put a small candle on each tray.

GENERAL COOKING TECHNIQUES

Sautéing

Sautéing is a form of quick frying, with no cover on the pan. In French, *sauter* means "to jump," which is what vegetables or small pieces of food do when you shake the sauté pan. The purpose is to brown the food lightly and seal in the juices, sometimes before further cooking. This technique has three critical elements: the right pan, the proper temperature, and dry food.

The sauté pan: A proper sauté pan is 10 to 12 inches in diameter and has 2- to 3-inch straight sides that allow you to turn the food and still keep the fat from spattering. It has a heavy bottom that can be moved back and forth easily across a burner.

The best material (and the most expensive) for a sauté pan is tin-lined copper because it is a superior heat conductor. Heavy-gauge aluminum works well but will discolor acidic food like tomatoes. Therefore, you should not use aluminum if acidic food is to be cooked for more than 20 minutes after the initial browning. Another option is to select a heavy-duty sauté pan made of strong, heat-conducting aluminum alloys. This type of professional cookware is smooth and stick resistant.

Use a sauté pan large enough to hold the food without crowding, or sauté in two batches. The heat of the fat and the air spaces around the pieces facilitate browning.

Many recipes call for sautéing first, then lowering the heat and cooking the food, covered, for an additional 10 to 20 minutes. Be sure you buy a sauté pan with a tight-fitting cover. Make certain the handle is long and is comfortable to hold. Use a wooden spatula or tongs to keep food moving in the pan as you shake it over the burner. If

---

Caviar

Like Champagne, caviar connotes luxurious living, but it is no longer strictly a luxury food. Many types of caviar are now priced to fit into an average budget, which allows people to serve it more often. In this volume, caviar is used in recipes for both appetizers and main courses; let your pocketbook dictate the type you use.

Genuine caviar is the roe, or eggs, of sturgeon from the Caspian Sea. The eggs vary in color from ivory and silver-gray to black, but their color has no bearing on their flavor. In recent years, pollution and overfishing have depleted the sturgeon supply, making its caviar both scarce and costly. To meet the demand for caviar, merchants from many countries are packaging eggs from other varieties of fish, such as salt-water salmon, whitefish, and lumpfish. By law, tins of these caviars must be marked with the name of the fish from which the eggs come to clearly indicate that the roe is not from the sturgeon. Therefore, a jar labeled LUMPFISH CAVIAR is not *true* caviar. For the purposes of this volume, however, we will call all fish roe caviar.

This brief guide introduces you to the varieties of caviar most commonly found in the American market. Imported caviars come both fresh and pasteurized, whereas most domestic caviars are available only pasteurized, a process that produces a slightly tougher product. The best sturgeon caviars are labeled MALASSOL (from the Russian word meaning "little salt"), which indicates that the eggs are preserved in only a minute amount of salt.

Beluga: The premium sturgeon caviar, these blue-gray eggs are large and firm but fragile, with a subtle flavor. Available by the ounce at some gourmet stores, beluga is about twice as expensive as other varieties of sturgeon caviar.

Oestra: Second in size to beluga, this sturgeon caviar is burnished gold to brown-black in color, with a delicate, nutlike flavor.

Sevruga: The least costly of sturgeon caviars, these tiny eggs, which are firmer than oestra or beluga, range in color from dark-gray to black.

Saltwater salmon: These inexpensive eggs from the Pacific salmon are clear to pinkish-orange and rather salty.

Lumpfish: This readily available, inexpensive domestic caviar consists of small, strongly flavored eggs dyed either red or black. It is not suitable for dishes in which appearance is important because the dye runs.

Whitefish: The bland, crunchy eggs from this freshwater fish are particularly good with pasta or potatoes.

Buying and Storing

Fresh caviar (or caviar that is not pasteurized) is sold in sealed tins and jars and from bulk containers. It requires constant, controlled refrigeration. If you are buying fresh caviar scooped from an already opened container, make sure the eggs are separate and unbroken, and of uniform color with no oily film on the surface. There should be no fishy aroma. Fresh caviar should not be bitter, overly salty, or chewy. Ask for a sample before you buy.

At home, fresh caviar should be stored in the refrigerator at between 32 and 40 degrees (its freezing point is 28 degrees), where it will last from one to four weeks. Freezing caviar turns the eggs to mush.

Pasteurized caviars, or lesser-quality eggs, have been partially cooked. These vacuum-sealed caviars have a longer shelf life than the fresh types: An unopened tin or jar lasts for two to four months in a cool dark place, or for six months in the refrigerator. After opening, the container should be re-sealed and stored in the refrigerator, where it will keep for one to two weeks.

Serving

Traditionally, fine caviar is presented in a glass bowl on a bed of cracked ice and is transferred with a silver spoon to unbuttered pieces of crustless white toast. Lesser grades are often enhanced by a sprinkling of lemon juice and sieved hard-cooked egg yolks and whites. But don't let these traditions constrain you. Experiment with new ways of serving caviar of all types: Add it to soups, as Sarah Belk Rian does on page 49, or to a simple vinaigrette dressing; spoon it over steak or use it in a caviar pie, as Margaret Fraser does in her Menu 1, page 96. Caviar is also good on canapés, as Charlotte Turgeon shows, page 89. No matter how you serve it, caviar makes a fine addition to any late-night meal.

the food sticks, a metal spatula will loosen it best. Turn the food so that all surfaces come into contact with the hot fat.

Never immerse the hot pan in cold water because this warps the metal. Allow the pan to cool slightly, then add water and let it sit until you are ready to wash it.

The fat: Half butter and half vegetable or peanut oil is perfect for most sautéing: It heats to high temperatures without burning, yet gives a rich butter flavor. For cooking, unsalted butter tastes best and adds no extra salt.

If you prefer an all-butter flavor, clarify the butter before you begin. This means removing the milky residue, which is the part that scorches. To clarify butter, heat it in a small saucepan over medium heat, and using a cooking spoon, skim off and discard the foam as it rises to the top. Keep skimming until no more foam appears. Pour off the remaining oil—the clarified butter—leaving the milky residue at the bottom of the pan. You may clarify only the amount of butter required for the meal you are preparing, or you may make a large quantity and store it in your refrigerator for two to three weeks, if desired.

Some sautéing recipes in this book call for olive oil, which imparts a delicious and distinctive flavor of its own and is less sensitive than butter to high heat. Nevertheless, even the finest olive oil has some residue of fruit pulp, which will occasionally scorch. Watch carefully when you sauté in olive oil; discard any scorched oil and start with fresh, if necessary.

To sauté properly, heat the fat until it is hot but not smoking. When you see small bubbles on top of the fat, lower the heat because it is on the verge of smoking. When using butter and oil together, add butter to the hot oil.

After the foam from the melting butter subsides, you are ready to sauté. If the temperature of the fat is just right, the food will sizzle when you put it in the pan. Charlotte Turgeon sautés chicken breasts, page 86.

Stir Frying

This technique requires very little oil, and the foods—which you stir continuously—fry quickly over very high heat. Stir frying is ideal for cooking bite-size, shredded, or thinly sliced portions of vegetables, fish, meat, or poultry, alone or in combination. Warren Mah stir fries carrots, snow peas, and mushrooms, page 77.

Braising

Braising is simmering meats or vegetables in a relatively small amount of liquid, usually for a long period of time. Sometimes the food is browned or parboiled before braising. You may wish to flavor the braising liquid with herbs, spices, and aromatic vegetables, or use wine, stock, or tomato sauce as a medium. Sarah Belk Rian braises red cabbage in red wine and Madeira, page 50.

Deglazing

This is an easy way to create a sauce for sautéed, braised, or roasted food. To deglaze, pour off all but 1 or 2 tablespoons of fat from the pan in which the food has been cooked. Add liquid—water, wine, or stock—and reduce the sauce over medium heat, using a wooden spoon to scrape up and blend into the sauce the concentrated juices and browned bits of food clinging to the bottom of the pan. Sara Belk Rian uses this technique when preparing chicken breasts, see page 52.

Coffee

Though wines and other alcoholic beverages may be served late at night, regular and decaffeinated coffees and coffee drinks are welcome nightcaps.

Three elements determine both the quality and taste of brewed coffee: the type of bean, the roasting time, and the brewing method. Roasting amplifies the inherent flavor and fragrance of green coffee beans. The length of roasting time determines the intensity of the beans' flavor. Light to medium roasts, which many Americans prefer, produce a mellow, delicate brew. Long-roasted beans produce the strong, robust coffees that Europeans and Middle Easterners drink. Italian espresso, produced from long-roasted beans, has a potent, almost burned taste.

Because characteristics vary, the type of coffee bean is another important determinant of taste. Colombian coffee beans produce a full-flavored yet delicate drink. By contrast, Sumatran Mandheling, Angolan, Mocha, Kenyan, or Brazilian beans are pungent and rich, and blend well with milder beans. Whether you buy whole roasted beans or commercially ground coffee, remember that both get stale quickly. Store beans and ground coffee in an airtight container in the refrigerator or freezer. They will retain flavor up to 4 months.

Whatever brewing method you use—percolator, drip, or vacuum—follow some basic rules. Metal pots can make coffee taste bitter, so use only glass or porcelain coffeemakers. Use freshly ground coffee from quality beans, and start with cold,

fresh water. Heat the water to just under the boiling point, about 205 degrees. If the water is at full boil, it extracts a bitter taste from the coffee grounds. Select the correct grind for your brewing method: Drip coffee requires a finer grind than percolated coffee. Serve coffee as soon as it is brewed, and do not reheat it.

For one cup of coffee, the standard ratio is 2 tablespoons of ground coffee to 1 cup of water. You may prefer a different strength, so experiment with proportions.

The following recipes are for special coffees:

Café au lait: Pour hot coffee and an equal amount of hot milk together into each cup or mug.

Espresso: Use espresso coffee that has been ground for use in American coffeemakers. Use 10 tablespoons ground espresso to 2½ cups of water. Serve the coffee with a strip of lemon zest, if desired.

Mocha: Pour equal amounts of hot coffee and hot chocolate into each cup. Sweeten to taste. Top with whipped cream and shaved bittersweet chocolate, if desired.

Mexican: Pour hot coffee into each cup and add a cinnamon stick. Top with whipped cream, if desired.

Irish: Put a teaspoonful of sugar, or more or less to taste, in the bottom of a stemmed heatproof glass. Add a jigger of Irish whiskey, then add hot coffee to within half an inch of the rim. Stir until the sugar dissolves. Slowly add heavy cream until the glass is filled.

Sparkling Wine

Sparkling wine—especially Champagne—adds a note of distinction to any occasion, especially to a late-night supper. Despite its luxurious image, a Champagne or a less costly sparkling wine goes well with most foods and is delicious drunk before, during, or after meals.

French Champagne is the aristocrat of sparkling wines. Blended from special grapes grown in a harmonious climate, it is carefully fermented to produce its renowned pinprick sparkle. By Common Market edict, only those sparkling wines produced from grapes grown on 60,000 acres in the region of Champagne in northeastern France are legitimately Champagne—with a capital C. Nothing else, not even the increasingly popular American sparkling wines, is Champagne, though the label may say so. Check the label on the bottle before buying sparkling wine for information on the producer and country of origin.

More than 85 percent of all French Champagnes are nonvintage, which means they are a blend of wine from the current year's harvest plus special reserve wines from earlier years. Nonvintage Champagne is of consistent quality and tastes the same year after year. Vintage Champagnes, which are costlier, are also blends but are made from wine of a single year's exceptional harvest. The year appears on the bottle.

Selecting a sparkling wine for a menu is a matter of personal taste, but the following categories should guide you:

Brut: This is the driest type of sparkling wine and the one most connoisseurs prefer. It is particularly good as an aperitif. It does not go well with a sweet dessert or with a strong cheese.

Extra-sec: This type is slightly less dry than brut and is recommended as a dessert drink, especially with fresh fruit or fruit desserts.

Sec and *demi-sec:* These types are sweeter and are often served in place of cocktails or with very sweet desserts.

Since the United States is not a Common Market member, domestic vintners often sell their sparkling wines as champagne because these wines are indeed produced by the traditional French *méthode champenoise*—which means they are allowed to develop their characteristic sparkle during a second fermentation in the bottle. Today, some top-grade sparkling wines (made by the *méthode champenoise*) are being produced in California and in New York State.

Several sparkling wines from Spain—from the Penedés area of Catalonia near Barcelona—are also made by the *méthode champenoise*, as are the Italian sparkling wines known as *spumante*. These wines have become increasingly popular with American consumers: Their low price tag is coupled with surprisingly high quality.

Although considerably less costly, imported and domestic sparkling burgundies are not recommended for late-night meals; imported sparkling rosés are occasionally good and should be served with food—not as an aperitif.

Before serving Champagne or any other sparkling wine, chill it properly—at least 30 minutes in a bucket of ice *and* ice water; ice alone is too cold. Or, chill the bottle in an uncrowded refrigerator (so the air can circulate around the bottle) for 4 to 5 hours. Avoid overchilling, and never freeze Champagne or sparkling wine.

To produce a soft pop when uncorking—and to prevent loss of wine—handle the bottle gently. Grasp it firmly in one hand and unwind and remove the wire muzzle with the other. Grip the cork and tilt the bottle slightly, then twist the bottle (not the cork) slowly in one direction until the cork slides out. If you perfect this technique and the bottle is properly chilled, there is no need to use a towel to cover the cork. Remember, though, to point the bottle away from people and anything breakable.

Always use tulip- or flute-shaped glasses when serving sparkling wine, and make sure they are carefully rinsed and wiped dry to remove any trace of dust or detergent. The slightest residue destroys the wine's sparkle.

When pouring wine, pour just a little into each glass. After the foam has subsided, fill the glasses two-thirds full. Never pour sparkling wine over ice cubes or into chilled glasses because the sudden cold will kill the bubbles. Count on 6 generous glasses of sparkling wine from a standard-size (750 ml.) bottle, and 1 to 2 glasses per person. Many sparkling wines come in splits (quarter bottles), half bottles, and magnums (a magnum is the equivalent of two bottles).

On those rare occasions when you do not consume all the sparkling wine, you can use a special re-corking device, sold at fine gourmet and houseware stores, to retain the effervescence of the sparkling wine for up to 48 hours. You can also use leftover sparkling wine in cooking as you would white wine.

Blanching

Blanching, or parboiling, is an invaluable technique. Immerse vegetables for a few minutes in boiling water, then refresh them, that is, plunge them into cold water to stop their cooking and set their colors. Blanching softens or tenderizes dense or crisp vegetables, often as a preliminary to further cooking by another method, such as stir frying. Victoria Fahey blanches spinach, page 18.

Broiling and Grilling

In broiling, the food cooks directly under the heat source. In grilling, the food cooks either directly over an open fire or on a well-seasoned cast-iron or stoneware griddle placed directly over a burner. Evelyne Slomon broils salmon in her Menu 2, page 31.

Roasting and Baking

Roasting is a dry-heat process, usually used for large cuts of meat and poultry, that cooks the food by exposing it to heated air in an oven or, perhaps, a covered barbecue. For more even circulation of heat, the food should be placed in a shallow pan or on a rack in a pan. For greater moisture retention, baste the food with its own juices, fat, or a flavorful marinade.

Baking applies to the dry-heat cooking of foods such as casseroles; small cuts of meat, fish, poultry, and vegetables; and of course, breads and pastries. Some foods are baked tightly covered to retain their juices and flavors; others, such as breads, cakes, and cookies, are baked in open pans to release moisture. Mary Cleaver bakes eggs with pasta and peppers, page 41.

Pantry (for this volume)

A well-stocked, properly organized pantry is essential for preparing great meals in the shortest time possible. Whether your pantry consists of a small refrigerator and two or three shelves over the sink, or a large freezer, refrigerator, and entire room just off the kitchen, you must protect staples from heat and light.

In maintaining your pantry, follow these rules:

1. Store staples by kind and date. Canned goods, canisters, and spices need a separate shelf, or a separate spot on a shelf. Date all staples—shelved, refrigerated, or frozen—by writing the date directly on the package or on a bit of masking tape. Then put the oldest ones in front to be sure you use them first.

2. Store flour, sugar, and other dry ingredients in canisters or jars with tight lids. Glass and clear plastic allow you to see at a glance how much remains.

3. Keep a running grocery list so that you can note when a staple is half gone, and be sure to stock up.

ON THE SHELF:

Anchovies
Anchovy fillets, both flat and rolled, come oil-packed, in tins. If you buy whole, salt-packed anchovies, they must be cleaned under running water, skinned, and boned. To bone, separate the fish with your fingers and slip out the backbone.

Baking powder

Capers
Capers are usually packed in vinegar and less frequently in salt. If you use the latter, you should rinse them under cold water before using them.

Cornstarch
Less likely to lump than flour, cornstarch is an excellent thickener for sauces. Substitute in the following proportions: 1 tablespoon cornstarch to 2 of flour.

Flour
all-purpose, bleached or
    unbleached
whole wheat

Garlic
Store in a cool, dry, well-ventilated place. Garlic powder and garlic salt are not adequate substitutes for fresh garlic.

Herbs and spices
The flavor of fresh herbs is much better than that of dried. Fresh herbs should be refrigerated and used as soon as possible. The following herbs are perfectly acceptable dried, but buy in small amounts, store airtight in dry area away from heat and light, and use as quickly as possible. In measuring herbs, remember that one part dried will equal three parts fresh. *Note:* Dried chives and parsley should not be on your shelf, since they have little or no flavor; frozen chives are acceptable. Buy whole spices rather than ground, as they keep their flavor much longer. Grind spices at home and store as directed for herbs.

basil
bay leaves
Cayenne pepper
chili powder
cinnamon
cloves, ground
coriander, whole and
    ground
cumin seeds, whole and
    ground
curry powder
dill
fennel seeds
mustard (powdered)
nutmeg, whole and ground
oregano
paprika
pepper
> *black peppercorns*
> These are unripe peppercorns dried in their husks. Grind with a pepper mill for each use.
> *white peppercorns*
> These are the same as the black variety, but are picked ripe and husked. Use them in pale sauces when black pepper specks would spoil the appearance.

rosemary
saffron
> Made from the dried stigmas of a species of crocus, this spice—the most costly of all seasonings—adds both color and flavor. Use sparingly.

sage
salt
> Use coarse salt—commonly available as kosher or sea—for its superior flavor, texture, and purity. Kosher salt and sea salt are less salty than table salt. Substitute in the following proportions: three-quarters teaspoon table salt equals just under one teaspoon kosher or sea salt.

tarragon
thyme
turmeric

Hot pepper sauce

Nuts
pine nuts (pignoli)

Oils
corn, safflower, peanut,
    or vegetable
> Because these neutral-tasting oils have high smoking points, they are good for high-heat sautéing.

olive oil
> Sample French, Greek, Spanish, and Italian oils. Olive oil ranges in color from pale yellow to dark green and in taste from mild and delicate to rich and fruity. Different olive oils can be used for different purposes: for example, stronger ones for cooking, lighter ones for salads. The finest quality olive oil is labeled extra-virgin or virgin.

sesame oil
> Dark amber-colored Oriental-style oil, used for seasoning; do not substitute light cold-pressed sesame oil.

Olives
California pitted black
    olives
Niçoise, Gaeta, or
    Kalamata olives

Onions
Store all dry-skinned onions in a cool, dry, well-ventilated place.

red or Italian onions
> Zesty tasting and generally eaten raw. The perfect salad onion.

shallots
> The most subtle member of the onion family, the shallot has a delicate garlic flavor.

Spanish onions
> Very large with a sweet flavor, they are best for stuffing and baking and are also eaten raw.

yellow onions
> All-purpose cooking onions, strong in taste.

Potatoes, boiling and
    baking
"New" potatoes are not a particular kind of potato, but any potato that has not been stored.

Rice
long-grain white rice
> Slender grains, much longer than they are wide, that become light and fluffy

when cooked and are best for general use.

Sesame seeds

Soy sauce

Japanese
  Lighter and less salty than Chinese and American brands.

Stock, chicken
  For maximum flavor and quality, your own stock is best (see recipe page 8), but canned stock, or broth, is adequate for most recipes and convenient to have on hand.

Sugar

granulated sugar

Tomatoes

Italian plum tomatoes
  Canned plum tomatoes (preferably imported) are an acceptable substitute for fresh.

Vinegars

balsamic vinegar

distilled white vinegar

red and white wine
  vinegars

rice vinegar

Wines and spirits

red wine, dry

sake

sherry, dry

vermouth, dry

white wine, dry

Water chestnuts

Worcestershire sauce

IN THE REFRIGERATOR:

Basil
  Though fresh basil is widely available only in summer, try to use it whenever possible to replace dried; the flavor is markedly superior. Stand the stems, preferably with roots intact, in a jar of water, and loosely cover leaves with a plastic bag.

Bread crumbs
  You need never buy bread crumbs. To make fresh crumbs, use fresh or day-old bread and process in food processor or blender. For dried, toast bread 30 minutes in preheated 250-degree oven, turning occasionally to prevent slices from browning.

Proceed as for fresh. Store bread crumbs in an airtight container: fresh crumbs in the refrigerator and dried crumbs in a cool, dry place. Either type may also be frozen for several weeks if tightly wrapped in a plastic bag.

Butter
  Many cooks prefer unsalted butter because of its finer flavor and because it does not burn as easily as salted.

Cheese

Cheddar cheese, sharp
  A firm cheese, ranging in color from nearly white to yellow. Cheddar is a versatile cooking cheese.

Goat cheese
  Goat cheese, or *chèvre*, has a distinct tanginess, though it is quite mild when young. Domestic goat cheeses are less salty than the imported types.

Parmesan cheese
  Avoid the pre-grated packaged variety; it is very expensive and almost flavorless. Buy Parmesan by the quarter- or half-pound wedge and grate as needed: 4 ounces produces about one cup of grated cheese.

Chili sauce

Chives
  Refrigerate fresh chives wrapped in plastic. You may also buy small pots of growing chives—keep them on a windowsill and snip as needed.

Coriander
  Also called *cilantro* or Chinese parsley, its pungent leaves resemble flat-leaf parsley. Keep in a glass of water covered with a plastic bag.

Cream

half-and-half

heavy cream

sour cream

Eggs
  Will keep 4 to 5 weeks in refrigerator. For best results, bring to room temperature before using, except when separating.

Ginger, fresh

Found in the produce section. Wrap in a paper towel, then in plastic, and refrigerate; it will keep for about 1 month, but should be checked weekly for mold. Or, if you prefer, store it in the freezer, where it will last about 3 months. Firm, smooth-skinned ginger need not be peeled.

Lemons
  In addition to its many uses in cooking, a slice of lemon rubbed over cut apples and pears will keep them from discoloring. Do not substitute bottled juice or lemon extract.

Limes

Milk

Mint
  Fresh mint will keep for a week if wrapped in a damp paper towel and enclosed in a plastic bag.

Mustards
  The recipes in this book usually call for Dijon or coarse-grained mustard.

Parsley
  The two most commonly available kinds of parsley are flat-leaf and curly; they can be used interchangeably when necessary. Flat-leaf parsley has a more distinctive flavor and is generally preferred in cooking. Curly parsley wilts less easily and is excellent for garnishing. Store parsley in a glass of water and cover loosely with a plastic bag. It will keep for a week in the refrigerator. Or wash and dry it, and refrigerate in a small plastic bag with a dry paper towel inside to absorb any moisture.

Scallions
  Scallions have a mild onion flavor. Store wrapped in plastic.

Tortillas

Yogurt

Equipment

Proper cooking equipment makes the work light and is a good cook's most prized possession. You can cook expertly without a store-bought steamer or even a food processor, but basic pans, knives, and a few other items are indispensable. Below are the things you need—and some attractive options—for preparing the menus in this volume.

Pots and pans
Large kettle or stockpot
3 skillets (large, medium, small) with covers; one with oven-proof handle
2 heavy-gauge sauté pans, 10 to 12 inches in diameter, with covers
3 saucepans with covers (1-, 2-, and 4-quart capacities)
  Choose heavy-gauge enameled cast-iron, plain cast-iron, aluminum-clad stainless steel, or aluminum (but you need at least one saucepan that is not aluminum). Best—but very expensive—is tin-lined copper.
Nonaluminum double boiler
14- to 16-inch wok
Broiler pan with rack
Shallow baking pan
  (13 x 9 x 2-inch)
Cookie sheet (15 x 10-inch)
Jelly-roll pan
Large ovenproof baking dish
Ovenproof serving platters
Four 8-ounce custard cups or ramekins
Salad bowl

Knives
A carbon-steel knife takes a sharp edge but tends to rust. You must wash and dry it after each use; otherwise it can blacken foods and counter tops. Good-quality stainless-steel knives, frequently honed, are less trouble and will serve just as well in the home kitchen. Never put a fine knife in the dishwasher. Rinse it, dry it, and put it away—but not loose in a drawer. Knives will stay sharp if they have their own storage rack.
Small paring knife
10-inch chef's knife
Sharpening steel

Other cooking tools
2 sets of mixing bowls in graduated sizes, one set preferably glass or stainless steel
Colander with a round base (stainless steel, aluminum, or enamel)
2 strainers in fine and coarse mesh
2 sets of measuring cups and spoons in graduated sizes
  One for dry ingredients, another for shortenings and liquids.
Mesh strainer
Slotted spoon
Long-handled wooden spoons
Ladle
Slotted spatula
2 metal spatulas or turners (for lifting hot foods from pans)
Rubber or vinyl spatula (for folding in ingredients)
Rolling pin
Grater (metal, with several sizes of holes)
  A rotary grater is handy for hard cheese.
Small wire whisk
Pair of metal tongs
Wooden board
Garlic press
Vegetable peeler
Vegetable brush
Mortar and pestle
Pastry brush for basting (a small, new paintbrush that is not nylon serves well)
Cooling rack
Kitchen shears
Kitchen timer
Cheesecloth
Aluminum foil
Paper towels
Plastic wrap
Waxed paper
Kitchen string
Oven mitts or potholders
Small brown paper bag
Thin rubber gloves

Electric appliances
Food processor or blender
  A blender will do most of the work required in this volume, but a food processor will do it more quickly and in larger volume. A food processor should be considered a necessity, not a luxury, for anyone who enjoys cooking.
Electric mixer

Optional cooking tools
Salad spinner
Butter warmer
Small jar with tight-fitting lid
Spice grinder
Icing spatula
Salad servers
Citrus juicer
  Inexpensive glass kind from the dime store will do.
Nutmeg grater
Zester
Deep-fat thermometer
2-inch biscuit cutter
Roll of masking tape or white paper tape for labeling and dating

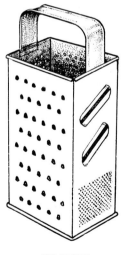

GRATER

COLANDER

STRAINER

FOOD PROCESSOR

RUBBER SPATULA

WHISK

MIXING BOWLS

METAL SPATULA

VEGETABLE PEELER

SHARPENING STEEL

CHEF'S KNIFE

DOUBLE BOILER

PARING KNIFE

TONGS

SLOTTED SPATULA

SAUCEPANS

SAUTÉ PAN

SKILLET

Victoria Fahey

MENU 1 (Right)
Mock Maki
White Rice

MENU 2
Herbed Pork Salad
Soufflé Roll with Apples and Calvados Cream

MENU 3
Bacon, Lettuce, and Tomato Salad
Pesto Toast
Oatmeal-Raisin Chocolate Chip Cookies

Victoria Fahey feels that late-night meals can be filling and nutritious without leaving guests overstuffed. When preparing a late supper, she takes full advantage of the seasonal fruits, vegetables, and seafood available at her local markets to produce dishes that are light and fresh tasting.

In Menu 1, she offers a variation on Japanese *makizushi*—vinegared rice and vegetables or fish rolled in seaweed. In her version, adapted to American ingredients and tastes, she rolls fillings of fruit, asparagus, scallops, shrimp, and cream cheese in wrappers of ham, spinach leaves, and smoked salmon. To save time, she eliminates the vinegared rice and offers boiled white rice on the side. Her mock *maki*, as she calls these bite-size morsels, are as aesthetically pleasing and nutritious as their Japanese counterparts.

To satisfy her preference for something warm and comforting late at night, in Menu 2 the cook prepares a classic egg *roulade*, or soufflé roll. Here, the flat soufflé encloses a filling of apples and is accompanied by a creamy sauce containing Calvados, the apple brandy of Normandy. You can serve the tart salad of greens and herbed pork as a first course, but if you do, wait to broil the soufflé roll until your guests have finished the salad.

Menu 3 is a good spur-of-the-moment meal because it utilizes ingredients you may have on hand in the refrigerator or freezer. A bacon, lettuce, and tomato salad is served with French bread topped with pesto sauce, and freshly baked chocolate chip cookies are the dessert.

Present a tempting array of mock maki *on traditional Japanese serving pieces, if you have them. Suggest that your guests use chopsticks—or their fingers—to help themselves to the ham-wrapped asparagus and kiwi, spinach-wrapped scallops and shrimp, and herbed cream cheese rolled in smoked salmon.*

16

Mock Maki
White Rice

This recipe for mock *maki* should inspire you to create your own variations. Try rolling trimmed scallions in thin slices of roast beef; cubes of melon or papaya and slices of preserved ginger in Westphalian or another fine smoked ham; or chunks of hard-boiled egg in slices of salami. Be sure to choose combinations with contrasting colors, textures, and flavors. Figure on about 12 pieces of mock *maki* per person. You can make these tidbits early in the day, but store them tightly wrapped in plastic in the refrigerator until serving time.

WHAT TO DRINK

To complement this Japanese-style supper, the cook suggests *sake* served hot or cold, a light Japanese beer, or *genmai cha*, a smoky-flavored green tea made with toasted rice kernels.

SHOPPING LIST AND STAPLES

12 sea scallops (about ¾ pound total weight)
16 very thin slices Westphalian ham (about ¾ pound total weight)
8 medium-size shrimp (about 6 ounces total weight)
4 slices smoked salmon (about ¼ pound total weight)
12 asparagus spears (about ¾ pound total weight)
1 bunch large-leaved spinach or beet greens (about 6 ounces)
Small bunch fresh dill, or ½ teaspoon dried
1 lemon
4 kiwi fruits, or 4 fresh figs
3-ounce package cream cheese
4 teaspoons Dijon mustard
4-ounce jar chopped pimientos
2-ounce jar red lumpfish caviar
1 cup long-grain white rice
Salt

UTENSILS

Medium-size skillet with cover
Large saucepan or stockpot
Medium-size heavy-gauge saucepan with cover
5 small serving platters or plates, or 2 large platters
3 small bowls
Colander
Large mesh strainer
Small strainer
Measuring cups and spoons
Chef's knife
Paring knife
Flexible-blade icing spatula or butter spreader

START-TO-FINISH STEPS

1. Follow maki recipe steps 1 through 15 and rice recipe step 1.
2. Follow maki recipe step 16 and rice recipe step 2.
3. While rice is cooking, follow maki recipe steps 17 through 24.
4. Follow rice recipe step 3.
5. Follow maki recipe steps 25 through 28, rice recipe step 4, and serve.

RECIPES

Mock Maki

8 medium-size shrimp (about 6 ounces total weight)
1 bunch large-leaved spinach or beet greens (about 6 ounces)
12 sea scallops (about ¾ pound total weight)
1 tablespoon salt
12 asparagus spears (about ¾ pound total weight)
4 kiwi fruits, or 4 fresh figs
16 very thin slices Westphalian ham (about ¾ pound total weight)
1 lemon
Small bunch fresh dill, or ½ teaspoon dried
3-ounce package cream cheese
4 slices smoked salmon (about ¼ pound total weight)
4 teaspoons Dijon mustard
2-ounce jar red lumpfish caviar
4-ounce jar chopped pimientos

1. Peel and devein shrimp: Pinch off legs several at a time, then bend back and snap off sharp, beaklike piece of shell just above tail. Remove shell and discard, leaving tail intact. Using sharp paring knife, make shallow incision along back of each shrimp, exposing black digestive vein. Extract black vein with your fingers and discard. Place shrimp in colander, rinse under cold water, and drain.
2. Bring 3 quarts of water to a boil in large saucepan or stockpot over high heat.
3. While water is heating, remove tough stems from spin-

ach or beet greens and wash leaves thoroughly in several changes of cold water. Remove and discard any bruised or discolored leaves. Set aside 20 of the largest leaves; reserve remainder for another use.

4. Add shrimp to boiling water and cook about 3 minutes, or just until they turn bright pink and become firm.

5. While shrimp are cooking, rinse scallops under cold running water; set aside.

6. Using large mesh strainer, transfer shrimp to colander and refresh under cold running water; keep water boiling in pan.

7. Add scallops to boiling water and cook 2 to 3 minutes, or until firm and opaque.

8. Meanwhile, drain shrimp and dry with paper towels. Transfer to small bowl, cover with plastic wrap, and refrigerate.

9. Using large mesh strainer, transfer scallops to colander and refresh under cold running water; keep water boiling in pan. Drain scallops and dry with paper towels. Transfer to small bowl, cover with plastic wrap, and refrigerate.

10. Drop spinach leaves into boiling water and blanch about 2 seconds, or just until slightly softened and bright green in color. Immediately turn spinach into colander and refresh under cold running water; set aside to drain.

11. In medium-size skillet, bring 3 to 4 cups water and 1 tablespoon salt to a boil over high heat.

12. Meanwhile, rinse asparagus under cold running water. Bend each spear and snap off stem end where natural break occurs; discard ends. Line up asparagus tips and trim bottoms so spears are of equal length.

13. Add asparagus to boiling water in skillet, cover, and cook 3 to 5 minutes, or until crisp-tender and bright green.

14. While asparagus is cooking, arrange spinach leaves in a single layer on double thickness of paper towels and dry. Cut out and discard center vein from each leaf; set leaves aside.

15. Transfer asparagus to colander and refresh under cold running water. Drain and dry with paper towels. Wrap in plastic and refrigerate.

16. Peel kiwis; if using figs, do not peel. To make kiwis or figs more cylindrical in shape, trim tops and bottoms. Halve each piece of fruit crosswise; set aside.

Kiwi fruit

17. Fold 1 slice of ham in half, then fold in uneven edges to form neat rectangular strip of same width as fruit. Wrap ham strip around 1 piece of fruit and transfer to a serving platter or plate; repeat for remaining fruit. Cover platter or plate with plastic wrap and refrigerate until ready to serve.

18. Halve lemon and squeeze enough juice from one half to measure 1 teaspoon. Cut remaining half crosswise into ¼-inch-thick slices; set aside.

19. Rinse fresh dill, if using, and pat dry with paper towels. Set aside 12 small sprigs for garnish and snip enough dill to measure 1 teaspoon; reserve remainder for another use.

20. Combine cream cheese, 1 teaspoon fresh or dried dill, and lemon juice in small bowl, and stir until blended.

21. Lay salmon flat on work surface and spread each slice with equal portion of cream cheese mixture. Starting with one long side, roll up each slice. Cut each long roll crosswise into thirds, transfer to a second platter or plate, and garnish each roll with a sprig of dill. Cover platter or plate with plastic wrap and refrigerate until ready to serve.

22. Lay out 2 slices of ham, overlapping 1 slice with half of the other; fold in uneven edges to form large rectangle of same length as asparagus spears. Spread 1 teaspoon mustard down length of rectangle. Gather up 3 asparagus spears and, beginning at long side of ham, roll ham tightly around bundle of asparagus. The meat should adhere to itself; if not, sprinkle lightly with cold water and roll again. Wrap the roll tightly in plastic and refrigerate until ready to serve. Repeat for remaining asparagus.

23. Turn caviar into small strainer and rinse gently under cold water until water runs clear. Set aside to drain.

24. Fold each of 12 spinach leaves lengthwise several times to form long strips having width equal to thickness of scallops. Wrap 1 spinach strip tightly around each scallop and transfer to third platter or plate. Top each scallop roll with ½ teaspoon caviar, cover platter or plate with plastic wrap, and refrigerate until ready to serve.

25. In small strainer, rinse 1 tablespoon chopped pimientos under cold running water; set aside to drain. Reserve remaining pimientos for another use.

26. Fold 8 remaining spinach leaves lengthwise into 1-inch-wide strips. Wrap 1 spinach strip tightly around middle of each shrimp and transfer to fourth platter or plate. Garnish each shrimp with a few bits of chopped pimiento, and garnish platter with lemon slices; set aside.

27. Remove asparagus rolls from refrigerator and unwrap. Cut each roll crosswise into thirds and transfer to fifth platter or plate.

28. Remove platters with salmon, scallop, and fruit maki from refrigerator and serve with shrimp and asparagus maki.

White Rice

1 teaspoon salt
1 cup long-grain white rice

1. In medium-size heavy-gauge saucepan, bring 2 cups of water and salt to a boil over high heat.

2. Add rice to boiling water, stir, and cover pan. Reduce heat to low and simmer gently 18 to 20 minutes, or until water is absorbed and rice is tender.

3. Remove pan from heat and set aside; do not remove cover.

4. When ready to serve, fluff rice with fork and divide among 4 small bowls.

Herbed Pork Salad
Soufflé Roll with Apples and Calvados Cream

A single rose gives an elegant touch to a tray with apple-filled soufflé roll and a mixed salad with herbed pork.

You can bake the soufflé and make the filling a day or two in advance and refrigerate or freeze them separately. If you plan to do this, make only half the amount of Calvados cream, and prepare the rest just before serving. Invert the flat soufflé onto a damp towel after baking and cover with another damp towel. Wrap the soufflé and towels tightly in foil and store in the freezer. When you are ready to fill and roll the soufflé, place the defrosted foil-wrapped package in a preheated 425-degree oven for about 5 minutes. Meanwhile, reheat the apple filling, then proceed with recipe step 21, and prepare Calvados cream. Or, you can bake, fill, and roll the soufflé a day ahead, wrap it tightly in foil, and refrigerate it. Before serving, reheat it in the foil for about 20 to 30 minutes in a 350-degree oven, then open the top of the foil, sprinkle on the cinnamon-sugar, and broil.

WHAT TO DRINK

A sparkling French or English cider would go nicely with this meal, as would a sweet, spicy wine such as a Riesling or Gewürztraminer.

SHOPPING LIST AND STAPLES

¾ pound ground pork
1 large or 2 small bunches arugula or watercress
1 head radicchio (about 6 ounces)
2 to 3 heads Belgian endive (about 6 ounces total weight)
Small bunch fresh thyme, or 1 teaspoon dried
4 to 6 tart apples, preferably Pippin or Granny Smith (about 2 pounds total weight)
6 eggs
1 cup milk
½ pint heavy cream
1 stick plus 4 tablespoons unsalted butter
1 tablespoon walnut or almond oil (optional)
1 tablespoon red wine vinegar
1 cup sugar, approximately
⅓ cup all-purpose flour
¾ teaspoon cinnamon
Pinch of ground cloves
¼ teaspoon nutmeg
Salt
Freshly ground pepper
2 tablespoons Calvados

UTENSILS

Large sauté pan, preferably nonstick, with cover
Medium-size skillet with cover
Medium-size saucepan
Small saucepan
Broiler pan with rack
Two 11 x 17-inch jelly-roll pans
2 large bowls
Medium-size nonaluminum bowl
Small bowl
Small jar with tight-fitting lid (if using oil for dressing)
Measuring cups and spoons
Chef's knife
Paring knife
2 wooden spoons
Slotted spoon
Metal spatula
Rubber spatula
Electric mixer or whisk
Kitchen towel

START-TO-FINISH STEPS

One hour ahead: Set out eggs to come to room temperature for soufflé roll.

1. Follow salad recipe steps 1 through 5.
2. Follow soufflé roll recipe steps 1 through 21.
3. Follow salad recipe steps 6 through 8 and serve.
4. Follow soufflé roll recipe steps 22 through 24 and serve.

RECIPES

Mixed Green Salad with Herbed Pork

1 large or 2 small bunches arugula or watercress
1 head radicchio (about 6 ounces)
2 to 3 heads Belgian endive (about 6 ounces total weight)
Small bunch fresh thyme, or 1 teaspoon dried
¾ pound ground pork
½ teaspoon salt
¼ teaspoon freshly ground pepper
1 tablespoon walnut or almond oil (optional)
1 tablespoon red wine vinegar

1. Wash arugula or watercress and dry with paper towels. Trim stems and discard. Remove and discard any bruised or discolored leaves. Place greens in large bowl; set aside.

Arugula

2. Rinse radicchio and dry with paper towels. Tear into bite-size pieces; add to greens.

Radicchio

21

3. Rinse endive and dry with paper towels. Trim stem ends. Cut crosswise into ½-inch-wide pieces; add to bowl with greens and radicchio. Cover bowl with plastic wrap and refrigerate until ready to serve.

4. Place 4 salad plates in refrigerator to chill.

5. If using fresh thyme, rinse and dry with paper towels. Strip enough leaves from stems to measure 1 teaspoon; set aside.

6. Combine ground pork, salt, pepper, and thyme in medium-size skillet and sauté, stirring, over high heat about 2 minutes, or until brown and crisp. Pour off fat, cover skillet, and set aside.

7. If using oil, combine oil and red wine vinegar in small jar with tight-fitting lid and shake until blended. Pour dressing or vinegar over salad and toss until evenly coated.

8. Divide salad among chilled salad plates. Using slotted spoon, top each salad with equal portion of pork mixture, and serve.

Soufflé Roll with Apples and Calvados Cream

Calvados cream:
1 cup heavy cream
3 tablespoons sugar
2 tablespoons Calvados

Filling:
4 to 6 tart apples, preferably Pippin or Granny Smith
  (about 2 pounds total weight)
1 stick unsalted butter
3 tablespoons sugar

Soufflé:
5 to 6 tablespoons sugar
1 cup milk
4 tablespoons unsalted butter
⅓ cup all-purpose flour
¾ teaspoon salt
½ teaspoon cinnamon
¼ teaspoon nutmeg
Pinch of ground cloves
6 eggs, at room temperature

Topping:
¼ teaspoon cinnamon
3 tablespoons sugar

1. Preheat oven to 425 degrees. Set oven rack in center of oven.

2. Combine cream, 3 tablespoons sugar, and Calvados in medium-size nonaluminum bowl; set aside to allow sugar to dissolve.

3. For filling, peel, halve, and core apples; cut lengthwise into ½-inch-thick slices. You will have approximately 5 to 6 cups.

4. Melt 1 stick butter over medium heat in large sauté pan. Increase heat to high, add apples, and sauté, stirring, about 2 minutes. Reduce heat to low, add 3 tablespoons sugar, and cook, uncovered, stirring occasionally, about 10

minutes, or until apples are tender but still retain their shape.

5. Meanwhile, oil 1 jelly-roll pan and line with waxed paper. Oil paper and sprinkle with 3 to 4 tablespoons sugar; set aside.

6. Prepare soufflé base: In small saucepan, warm 1 cup milk over medium heat.

7. While milk is warming, melt 4 tablespoons butter in medium-size saucepan over high heat, and cook 1 minute, or until butter browns.

8. Reduce heat under butter to medium, stir in flour, and cook 2 minutes, stirring, until flour is slightly browned. Add ½ teaspoon salt and spices, and stir until blended.

9. Add warmed milk to mixture, ⅓ cup at a time, stirring after each addition until blended. Remove pan from heat; set aside.

10. Separate eggs, dropping whites into large bowl and yolks into small bowl.

11. Off heat, add yolks, one at a time, to soufflé base, stirring after each addition until blended; set aside.

12. With electric mixer or whisk, beat whites until foamy. Add remaining ¼ teaspoon salt, and continue to beat until stiff but not dry.

13. Using rubber spatula, fold one quarter of beaten egg whites into soufflé base. Gently fold in remaining whites.

14. Using thin-bladed knife, spread mixture evenly in prepared jelly-roll pan and bake about 10 minutes, or until firm. Do *not* overbake.

15. Meanwhile, stir Calvados cream to recombine. Measure out ½ cup; set remainder aside.

16. Increase heat under apples to medium-high and cook, stirring constantly, about 7 minutes, or until apples begin to caramelize.

17. Add ½ cup Calvados cream to apples and cook, stirring, 1 minute, or until most of the liquid evaporates. Cover pan, remove from heat, and set aside.

18. Spread kitchen towel over back of second jelly-roll pan and sprinkle towel with remaining 2 tablespoons sugar.

19. Remove soufflé from oven and set aside to cool slightly; then carefully invert onto towel-covered pan and peel off waxed paper.

20. Place broiler rack 6 inches from heating element and preheat broiler.

21. For topping, combine ¼ teaspoon cinnamon and 3 tablespoons sugar in measuring cup; set aside.

22. Using back of spoon, spread apple filling over flat soufflé, leaving ½-inch margin around edges. Starting at one narrow end, roll up soufflé, using towel to help you roll. Transfer soufflé roll, seam-side down, to baking sheet. Sprinkle with cinnamon-sugar and broil 1 minute, or until sugar begins to melt.

23. Meanwhile, whisk remaining Calvados cream until slightly thick but still runny; set aside.

24. Remove soufflé roll from broiler and cut into 4 slices. Spoon equal portions of Calvados cream onto 4 plates. Using metal spatula, place a slice of soufflé roll, sugar-crust side up, onto sauce on each plate and serve.

Bacon, Lettuce, and Tomato Salad
Pesto Toast
Oatmeal-Raisin Chocolate Chip Cookies

Top off an evening of games with a bacon, lettuce, and tomato salad, pesto toast, and freshly baked cookies.

Pesto, which originated in Genoa, is a classic Italian sauce. Here it tops wedges of toasted bread. If you do not have a food processor or blender, you can easily make pesto the traditional way with a mortar and pestle or by chopping the ingredients in a bowl.

If you want, double the recipe for the cookies and freeze some of the dough; this way you can quickly produce enough cookies for a crowd or just a few for yourself anytime the craving arises. To prepare the dough for the freezer, place heaping tablespoonsful about half an inch apart on cookie sheets or flat plates, and flatten each mound slightly with your fingertips. Place the cookie sheets or plates in the freezer until the dough firms (about 30 minutes), then carefully lift the cookies off with a spatula and put them in small plastic freezer bags. The dough will keep in the freezer for up to six months. Bake the cookies in a 350-degree oven until golden.

WHAT TO DRINK

With this light meal, serve cold milk, flavored with chocolate if you like, or perhaps hot chocolate. If you prefer wine, a soft one such as an Orvieto or a French Colombard would be good.

SHOPPING LIST AND STAPLES

1 pound thick-cut bacon
2 heads green leaf, Boston, or romaine lettuce
2 medium-size tomatoes (about 1 pound total weight),
    or 2 pints cherry tomatoes
1 clove garlic
Small bunch basil
1 lemon
2 extra-large or jumbo eggs
1 stick unsalted butter, approximately
¼ pound Cheddar cheese
¼ pound Parmesan cheese
¾ cup vegetable oil
2 tablespoons olive oil
1 teaspoon Dijon mustard
2-ounce jar pine nuts
1 baguette, or 4 to 8 thin slices home-style white bread
1½ cups oatmeal
15-ounce box dark or golden raisins
6-ounce package semisweet chocolate chips
1 cup brown sugar
½ cup granulated sugar
½ cup all-purpose flour
½ teaspoon baking soda
½ teaspoon cinnamon
½ teaspoon vanilla extract
Salt and freshly ground pepper

UTENSILS

Food processor or blender
Medium-size skillet
Broiler pan with rack
Two 17 x 11-inch cookie sheets
2 wire cooling racks
Salad bowl
Large bowl or mixer bowl
2 small bowls
Small jar with tight-fitting lid
Measuring cups and spoons
Chef's knife
Paring knife
2 wooden spoons
Slotted spoon
Wide metal spatula
Rubber spatula
Whisk
Mortar and pestle (if not using processor)
Grater (if not using processor)
Electric mixer

START-TO-FINISH STEPS

One hour ahead: Set out 1 egg and butter to come to room temperature for cookie recipe.

1. Follow cookie recipe steps 1 through 7.

2. While cookies are baking, follow salad recipe steps 1 through 6.
3. Follow cookie recipe step 8 and salad recipe steps 7 through 9.
4. Follow pesto toast recipe steps 1 through 7.
5. While bread is toasting, follow salad recipe step 10.
6. Follow pesto toast recipe step 8.
7. Follow salad recipe steps 11 and 12, and serve with pesto toast.
8. Follow cookie recipe step 9 and serve for dessert.

RECIPES

Bacon, Lettuce, and Tomato Salad

2 heads green leaf, Boston, or romaine lettuce
1 pound thick-cut bacon
2 medium-size tomatoes (about 1 pound total weight),
    or 2 pints cherry tomatoes
1 lemon
¼ pound Cheddar cheese

Mayonnaise:
Extra-large or jumbo egg
1 teaspoon Dijon mustard
1 teaspoon salt
½ teaspoon freshly ground pepper
¾ cup vegetable oil

1. Wash and dry lettuce. Remove and discard any bruised or discolored leaves. Reserve 12 whole leaves; shred remaining lettuce. Place whole leaves and shredded lettuce in salad bowl, cover, and refrigerate. Place 4 dinner plates in refrigerator to chill.

Romaine lettuce

2. Line plate with double thickness of paper towels; set aside.
3. Cut bacon into 1-inch-wide pieces. In medium-size skillet, fry bacon over medium heat 3 to 4 minutes, or until crisp.
4. While bacon is frying, wash tomatoes and dry with paper towels. Core and cut tomatoes into bite-size pieces, or halve cherry tomatoes, if using. Set aside.
5. Squeeze enough lemon juice to measure 1 tablespoon; set aside.
6. With slotted spoon, transfer bacon to paper-towel-lined plate to drain. Pour off all but 1 tablespoon fat from skillet; set skillet aside.
7. Using food processor fitted with shredding disk, or grater, shred cheese; transfer cheese to small bowl and set aside.
8. Prepare mayonnaise: Combine whole egg, mustard, salt, and pepper in container of food processor or blender and process at high speed for 1 minute, or until well

blended. With machine running, drizzle in oil and continue to process until oil is totally incorporated and mixture is thick and smooth. Measure out ¼ cup of the mayonnaise; transfer remainder to tightly covered jar and refrigerate for another use.

9. Add mayonnaise to bacon fat in skillet and whisk until well blended; set aside.

10. Remove whole lettuce leaves from bowl and divide among 4 dinner plates.

11. Add dressing, tomatoes, half of the bacon, and half of the cheese to shredded lettuce in bowl, and toss to combine. Taste and adjust seasoning, if necessary.

12. Divide salad among lettuce-lined plates and garnish with remaining bacon and cheese.

Pesto Toast

Small bunch basil
1 clove garlic
¼ pound Parmesan cheese
2 tablespoons olive oil
2 tablespoons pine nuts
1 baguette, or 4 to 8 thin slices home-style white bread

1. Preheat broiler.

2. Wash basil and dry with paper towels. Strip enough leaves from stems to measure 1 cup, firmly packed; set aside.

3. Peel and coarsely chop garlic; set aside.

4. Using food processor fitted with steel blade or on coarse side of grater, grate enough Parmesan to measure ½ cup; set aside.

5. Combine basil, garlic, olive oil, and 1 tablespoon pine nuts in bowl of food processor and process just until solid ingredients are coarsely chopped; do *not* overprocess. Or, using mortar and pestle, grind solid ingredients into a paste, then add oil and stir to combine. Transfer mixture to small bowl.

6. Add Parmesan to basil mixture and stir to combine.

7. Halve baguette lengthwise and then cut each half crosswise into 4- to 6-inch-wide pieces. Arrange bread, cut-sides up, in single layer on broiler rack and broil 6 inches from heating element until toasted.

8. Remove bread from broiler. Spread each slice with an equal amount of pesto, sprinkle with remaining pine nuts, and broil another minute, or until pine nuts are golden brown.

Oatmeal-Raisin Chocolate Chip Cookies

1 stick unsalted butter, approximately, at room
    temperature
½ cup granulated sugar
1 cup brown sugar, firmly packed
Extra-large or jumbo egg, at room temperature
½ teaspoon vanilla extract
½ teaspoon baking soda
½ teaspoon salt
½ teaspoon cinnamon

½ cup all-purpose flour
1½ cups oatmeal
1 cup dark or golden raisins
6-ounce package semisweet chocolate chips

1. Preheat oven to 350 degrees.

2. Grease two 17 x 11-inch cookie sheets; set aside.

3. Combine butter, granulated sugar, and brown sugar in large bowl or mixer bowl; beat with electric mixer on high speed 2 minutes, or until well blended and fluffy.

4. Add egg, ½ cup water, vanilla, baking soda, salt, and cinnamon to butter-sugar mixture, and beat on low speed just until combined. (Mixture may look curdled; this is fine.)

5. Add flour and oatmeal, and stir with wooden spoon to combine.

6. Stir in raisins and chocolate chips.

7. Drop dough by heaping tablespoonsful about 3 inches apart on prepared cookie sheets and bake 10 to 12 minutes, or until firm and golden brown. For crisper cookies, bake a few minutes longer.

8. Remove cookies from oven and set aside to cool for a few minutes on sheets. Using wide metal spatula, carefully remove cookies to racks to cool further.

9. Remove cookies from racks and serve. This recipe makes about 2 dozen cookies.

ADDED TOUCH

Cassis, a black currant syrup, is a natural partner for the blueberries in this simple sorbet. Be sure to use cassis syrup and not *crème de cassis*, the currant liqueur; the alcohol in the liqueur inhibits freezing.

Blueberry Cassis Sorbet

2 pints fresh blueberries, or 10-ounce package
    frozen unsweetened
1 lemon
½ cup granulated sugar
½ cup cassis, plus 1 tablespoon for garnish (optional)

1. If using fresh berries, place in colander and gently rinse. Remove and discard any bad berries. Turn berries onto paper towels to drain.

2. Squeeze enough lemon juice to measure 1 tablespoon.

3. Combine 1 cup water and ½ cup sugar in small saucepan and bring to a boil over high heat. Boil 1 minute, remove pan from heat, and set aside to cool.

4. Reserve ¼ cup whole berries. Combine remaining berries, ½ cup cassis, lemon juice, and cooled sugar syrup in food processor or blender and process until smooth.

5. Pour purée into 8-inch metal cake pan and freeze 2 hours.

6. Place 4 goblets or bowls in refrigerator to chill.

7. Remove sorbet from freezer 10 minutes before serving to soften.

8. Divide sorbet among chilled goblets or bowls. Top each serving with reserved berries, sprinkle with a little cassis, if desired, and serve.

Evelyne Slomon

T he food of Provence, in southeast France, has always captivated Evelyne Slomon. She spent every summer of her childhood in Cannes, the famed coastal resort, where each day centered around a large, leisurely noontime meal. At night, the food was light and often prepared ahead of time with minimum fuss. The dishes she presents here are her adaptations of traditional Provençal recipes. Because nearly all of them can be made early in the day and reheated later, or even served cold, they are ideal time-saving late-night fare.

Menu 1 features a variation on *poulet à la Niçoise*, which combines chicken and vegetables with Niçoise olives, garlic, olive oil, and herbs. Rather than sautéing a cut-up chicken in a heavy stockpot, Evelyne Slomon wraps chicken breasts and vegetables in individual foil packets and bakes them. Herbed rice topped with toasted pine nuts is the accompaniment.

In Menu 2, she spreads salmon scallops with an herb paste called *pistou* and then broils them. A classic Provençal *pistou* is made from herbs and garlic blended with fruity olive oil and sometimes grated cheese. It is often beaten into soups or used as a topping for vegetables, meat, and fish.

Menu 3 is a typical French family meal: A composed salad of chicory, red peppers, potatoes, and anchovies precedes a goat cheese and herb soufflé. The texture of this soufflé is more like that of a custard or quiche because beaten whole eggs are used rather than just the whites. With the soufflé, the cook serves tomato *coulis*, a chunky sauce flavored with garlic, onion, and fresh thyme.

Chicken breasts steamed with vegetables and Niçoise olives are especially delicious served with herbed rice to absorb the juices. For dessert, offer individual ramekins of baked fruits mixed with grated ginger and crushed almond cookies.

Chicken Niçoise in Packets
Herbed Rice with Pine Nuts
Fruit Gratin

As the skinless, boneless chicken breasts steam in foil packets with peppers, squash, tomatoes, orange zest, and herbs, the diverse flavors of the ingredients meld. When you are ready to serve the chicken, you may prefer to bring the packets to the table unopened. This way guests can unfold their own and enjoy the mouth-watering aromas. You can prepare this recipe up to eight hours in advance of serving and refrigerate the wrapped packets until cooking time. Or, you can bake them until done, poke a hole in each so the steam escapes, then refrigerate the chicken and vegetables, and serve cold.

A fruity, green extra-virgin olive oil is used in the rice dish. The color of the rice will depend upon the olive oil you select. To vary this recipe, dress the cooked rice with lemon juice and serve it as a salad, or use the rice to stuff vegetables such as tomatoes or zucchini.

WHAT TO DRINK

A good choice with this meal would be an assertive white wine such as a Sauvignon Blanc, whether it comes from California, Italy, or from France's Loire Valley.

SHOPPING LIST AND STAPLES

2 skinless, boneless chicken breasts, halved (about 2 pounds total weight)
4 large ripe tomatoes (about 3 pounds total weight)
1 pound yellow squash or zucchini
2 small green, red, or yellow bell peppers
2 heads garlic
2-inch piece fresh ginger
1 bunch fresh parsley
1 bunch fresh thyme, or 1¼ teaspoons dried
4 medium-size firm freestone peaches (about 1 pound total weight)
4 large plums (about ¾ pound total weight)
Large thick-skinned orange
1 pint vanilla ice cream (optional)
½ cup plus 2 tablespoons fruity, green extra-virgin olive oil, approximately
8¾-ounce jar Niçoise or oil-cured black olives
1 cup long-grain white rice
½ pound almond cookies
2-ounce jar pine nuts
1 tablespoon sugar, approximately
1 bay leaf

2 teaspoons fennel seeds
Salt and freshly ground black pepper
1 cup dry red wine
½ cup dry white vermouth or other dry white wine

UTENSILS

Small heavy-gauge saucepan
Medium-size heavy-gauge saucepan with cover
Two 17 x 11-inch baking sheets
2 small bowls
Four 6-inch ramekins or ceramic tartlets
8-ounce custard cup or ramekin
Strainer
Measuring cups and spoons
Chef's knife
Paring knife
Wooden spoon
Slotted spoon
Wide metal spatula
Vegetable brush
Pastry brush
Grater
Kitchen string
Cheesecloth (if using dried thyme)

START-TO-FINISH STEPS

1. Wash and dry parsley, and fresh thyme if using. Trim off stems from parsley and discard. Set aside 8 sprigs for chicken recipe, if desired, and 4 sprigs for rice recipe; reserve remainder for another use. Set aside 8 thyme sprigs for chicken recipe and 3 sprigs for rice recipe.
2. Follow chicken recipe steps 1 through 13.
3. Follow fruit gratin recipe steps 1 through 6.
4. While chicken and fruit gratins are baking, follow rice recipe steps 1 through 4.
5. Follow fruit gratin recipe step 7.
6. Follow rice recipe steps 5 and 6, chicken recipe step 14, and serve.
7. Follow fruit gratin recipe step 8 and serve as dessert.

RECIPES

Chicken Niçoise in Packets

2 tablespoons fruity, green extra-virgin olive oil
2 small green, red, or yellow bell peppers

2 heads garlic
Large thick-skinned orange
1 pound yellow squash or zucchini
4 large ripe tomatoes (about 3 pounds total weight)
2 skinless, boneless chicken breasts, halved (about
  2 pounds total weight)
1 cup Niçoise or oil-cured black olives
Salt and freshly ground black pepper
2 teaspoons fennel seeds
8 sprigs fresh thyme, or 1 teaspoon dried
8 sprigs fresh parsley (optional)
½ cup dry white vermouth or other dry white wine

1. Preheat oven to 500 degrees.
2. Bring 3 cups water to a boil in small saucepan over medium-high heat.
3. While water is heating, oil four 18 x 12-inch sheets of aluminum foil, leaving a 1-inch border unoiled.
4. Wash and dry bell peppers. Core and seed peppers. Cut crosswise into ¼-inch-thick rings; set aside.
5. Separate garlic into cloves, but do *not* peel. Add garlic to boiling water and cook 2 to 3 minutes.
6. Meanwhile, wash orange and dry with paper towel. Using paring knife, cut eight ½-inch-wide by 2-inch-long strips of zest, avoiding white pith.
7. Turn garlic into strainer; set aside.
8. Scrub squash with vegetable brush and rinse under cold running water. Trim ends and discard. Cut squash crosswise into ¼-inch-thick slices; set aside.
9. Wash tomatoes and dry with paper towels. Core and cut each tomato into thin wedges; set aside.
10. Wash chicken and dry with paper towels; set aside.
11. Divide squash among foil sheets, arranging slices in a single layer. Distribute half the green pepper rings, half the tomato wedges, half the olives, and half the garlic cloves over squash. Season each portion with salt and pepper to taste, sprinkle with half the fennel seeds, and top each with 2 sprigs fresh thyme and 1 strip orange zest. Layer each portion with 1 chicken breast half and remaining orange zest, green pepper rings, tomatoes, olives, and unpeeled garlic, in that order. Sprinkle with salt and pepper to taste and remaining fennel seeds, garnish with remaining thyme, and parsley if using, and drizzle with vermouth.
12. Gather up long ends of each foil sheet and fold over twice; fold up short ends, forming packages, and transfer to baking sheet.
13. Reduce oven temperature to 450 degrees, place chicken in oven, and bake 40 to 45 minutes, depending on thickness of breasts.
14. Remove baking sheet from oven. Carefully unfold each package, reserving juices, and, using wide metal spatula, transfer chicken and vegetables to dinner plate. Pour juices left in foil over each portion and serve.

Herbed Rice with Pine Nuts

3 sprigs fresh thyme or ¼ teaspoon dried
8 sprigs fresh parsley

1 bay leaf
½ cup fruity, green extra-virgin olive oil, approximately
2 tablespoons pine nuts
1 cup long-grain white rice
¼ teaspoon salt

1. If using fresh thyme, gather up thyme, 4 sprigs parsley, and bay leaf, and tie with kitchen string for bouquet garni. If using dried thyme, tie up herbs in square of cheesecloth; set aside.
2. Heat ¼ cup oil in medium-size heavy-gauge saucepan over medium heat. Add pine nuts and sauté, stirring, 1 to 2 minutes, or until light golden. Using slotted spoon, transfer nuts to small bowl and set aside; reserve oil in pan.
3. Add rice to pan and sauté over medium heat, stirring, about 1 minute, or until all the oil is absorbed and the rice begins to turn translucent.
4. Add 2 cups water, salt, and bouquet garni and stir to combine. Cover pan and simmer gently over low heat about 15 minutes, or until all the liquid is absorbed.
5. When rice is done, remove and discard bouquet garni. Drizzle with 2 tablespoons olive oil and toss with fork until evenly coated.
6. Generously oil 8-ounce custard cup and pack with rice, pressing gently with back of spoon to compress the rice. Quickly invert custard cup onto dinner plate and rap gently to dislodge molded rice. Repeat for remaining rice. Sprinkle each serving with toasted pine nuts and garnish with a sprig of parsley.

Fruit Gratin

½ pound almond cookies
2-inch piece fresh ginger
4 medium-size firm freestone peaches (about 1 pound total weight)
4 large plums (about ¾ pound total weight)
1 cup dry red wine
1 tablespoon sugar, approximately
1 pint vanilla ice cream (optional)

1. Coarsely crumble cookies into small bowl; set aside.
2. Grate enough ginger to measure 2 teaspoons. Distribute among 4 ramekins.
3. Halve peaches and plums lengthwise, cutting around pit. Holding each piece of fruit with both hands, gently rotate halves in opposite directions to separate. Using paring knife or your fingers, remove pits and discard. Cut each piece of fruit into 8 wedges.
4. Alternate peach and plum slices over ginger to resemble flower petals and place ramekins on baking sheet.
5. Pour ¼ cup wine over each serving, sprinkle with sugar to taste, and top with crumbled cookies.
6. Bake in preheated 450-degree oven 30 minutes, or until topping is crusty and wine is reduced to syrup-like consistency.
7. Remove desserts from oven and set aside until ready to serve.
8. Just before serving, top each dessert with a scoop of vanilla ice cream, if desired.

Broiled Salmon with Pistou
Noodles with Pine Nuts, Garlic, and Lemon
Baked Apple-Nougat Custard

Broiled salmon scallops make a simple yet elegant meal. You can use another firm-fleshed fish such as halibut or swordfish, but both may require longer cooking, depending on thickness. Allow 10 minutes per inch. To test for doneness, insert the tip of a sharp knife into the fish. It is done when the flesh is opaque and barely flakes.

WHAT TO DRINK

These dishes demand a full-bodied and flavorful white

Thin scallops of salmon topped with a richly textured herb paste and accompanied by noodles in a zesty lemon and garlic sauce make a light yet satisfying meal. To further delight your guests, offer an apple-nougat custard for dessert.

wine. Try a good French wine, such as a Châteauneuf-du-Pape from the Rhone, an Italian Gavi from the Piedmont, or a Greco di Tufo from Campania.

SHOPPING LIST AND STAPLES

Eight ¼- to ½-inch-thick salmon scallops, 1½ to 2 inches wide, with skin (about 2 pounds total weight)
2 cloves garlic
Small bunch each parsley, basil, and mint, or any combination
2 lemons
3 tart apples, such as Granny Smith (about 1 pound total weight)
3 eggs

1 cup milk
½ pint heavy cream (optional)
3 tablespoons unsalted butter, approximately
1 pound fresh or dried egg noodles
1 cup olive oil, approximately
5-ounce bag pine nuts
½ pound nougat candy
Salt and freshly ground pepper

UTENSILS

Food processor or blender
Stockpot
12 x 9 x 2-inch flameproof baking pan
12-inch oval or round baking dish
15 x 10-inch baking sheet
Large bowl
Medium-size bowl
Small bowl, plus additional bowl (if using whipped cream)
Colander
Measuring cups and spoons
Chef's knife
Paring knife
2 wooden spoons
Metal spatula

Rubber spatula
Grater (if not using processor)
Electric mixer (if using whipped cream)

START-TO-FINISH STEPS

Thirty minutes ahead: Place nougat candy in freezer to facilitate chopping.

1. Follow custard recipe steps 1 through 8.
2. Follow salmon recipe steps 1 through 5.
3. Follow noodles recipe steps 1 through 7.
4. Follow custard recipe step 9 and salmon recipe step 6.
5. Follow noodles recipe steps 8 through 10.
6. Follow salmon recipe steps 7 and 8, and serve with noodles.
7. Follow custard recipe steps 10 and 11, and serve as dessert.

RECIPES

Broiled Salmon with Pistou

Small bunch each parsley, basil, and mint, or any
  combination
½ cup olive oil, approximately

Eight ¼- to ½-inch-thick salmon scallops, 1½ to 2 inches wide, with skin (about 2 pounds total weight)
Salt and freshly ground pepper

1. Wash fresh herbs and pat dry with paper towels. Strip enough leaves from stems to measure ¾ cup firmly packed; reserve remaining herbs for another use.
2. In food processor fitted with steel blade, or in blender, finely mince herbs. With machine running, add oil in a slow, steady stream. Process 1 to 2 minutes, or until mixture is smooth and pastelike. Continue to process another 1 to 2 minutes. Turn pistou into small bowl.
3. Grease shallow flameproof baking pan with olive oil.
4. Rinse salmon and dry with paper towels.
5. Transfer salmon to prepared pan, arranging them in a single layer, skin-side down. Season lightly with salt and pepper to taste and, using the back of a spoon, spread each scallop with 1 tablespoon pistou; set aside.
6. Preheat broiler. Set rack 6 inches from heating element.
7. Place salmon in broiler and broil 3 to 5 minutes, or until flesh turns pale pink and slightly opaque.
8. Remove salmon from broiler and divide among dinner plates.

Noodles with Pine Nuts, Garlic, and Lemon

1 cup pine nuts
2 cloves garlic
1 lemon
Salt and freshly ground pepper
½ cup olive oil
1 pound fresh or dried egg noodles

1. Arrange pine nuts on baking sheet in a single layer and toast in preheated 400-degree oven, shaking pan occasionally to prevent scorching, 5 minutes, or until light brown.
2. Under flat blade of chef's knife, crush garlic; remove and discard peels.
3. Wash and dry lemon. Using paring knife or grater, remove zest, avoiding white pith as much as possible; chop finely. Set aside.
4. Remove pine nuts from oven and set aside to cool.
5. Combine 4 quarts of water and 1 tablespoon salt in stockpot and bring to a boil over high heat.
6. Combine garlic, lemon zest, and toasted pine nuts in food processor fitted with steel blade, or in blender, and

process until paste-like. Add salt and pepper to taste.
7. With machine running, add oil in a slow, steady stream and continue processing for 1 minute after oil has been added; set aside.
8. Add noodles to boiling water and cook 2 minutes for fresh, according to package directions for dried, or just until *al dente*. Just before noodles are done, add 1½ cups of the pasta cooking water to the sauce and process to blend; set aside.
9. Turn noodles into colander to drain.
10. Return noodles to stockpot, add sauce, and toss to combine. Cover pot and set aside until ready to serve.

Baked Apple-Nougat Custard

3 tablespoons unsalted butter, approximately
1 lemon
½ pound nougat candy, well chilled
3 tart apples, such as Granny Smith (about 1 pound)
3 eggs
1 cup milk
½ cup heavy cream (optional)

1. Preheat oven to 400 degrees. If using whipped cream for topping, put small bowl and beaters in freezer to chill.
2. Butter 12-inch baking dish and set aside.
3. Juice lemon; set aside.
4. Using food processor fitted with steel blade, or with chef's knife, coarsely chop nougat candy; set aside.
5. Peel, halve, and core apples.
6. Using food processor fitted with shredding disk, or on coarse side of grater, shred apples.
7. Combine apples, lemon juice, and 1 cup of the nougat in buttered dish and toss to combine. Smooth out top of mixture; set aside.
8. In medium-size bowl, beat eggs with fork until combined. Add milk and stir with fork until blended; pour over the apple mixture. Dot custard with 2 tablespoons butter, sprinkle with remaining nougat, and bake 40 to 45 minutes, or until golden and puffy.
9. Remove custard from oven, cover loosely with foil, and set aside.
10. When ready to serve, if using whipped cream, pour cream into chilled bowl and beat with electric mixer until cream stands in soft peaks.
11. Slice custard into wedges and serve with whipped cream, if desired.

Mixed Vegetable and Anchovy Salad
Herbed Chèvre Soufflé with Tomato Coulis

Wedges of goat cheese soufflé contrast in color and flavor with tomato coulis. A vegetable salad is the first course.

This unusual cheese soufflé gets its flavor from sharp-tasting goat cheese, which melts smoothly into the egg mixture. Select an imported French variety, such as Bucheron or Montrachet, or a tangy domestic one such as chabis. Goat cheeses are highly perishable and should be tightly wrapped in plastic and refrigerated if not being used immediately. The soufflé can be served hot or cold, unmolded or directly from the soufflé dish. When cold, its texture resembles that of cheesecake.

Consider making several batches of the tomato *coulis.* It stores well in the refrigerator for up to a week, can be frozen for up to six months, and is a fine base for tomato soup.

WHAT TO DRINK

A crisp, acidic white would be good with the soufflé. The cook suggests a California Sauvignon Blanc or a French wine from the Graves district. Italian Pinot Grigio would also be fine.

SHOPPING LIST AND STAPLES

2 medium-size ripe tomatoes (about 1 pound total weight), or 28-ounce can whole plum tomatoes
Medium-size head chicory (about 1¼ pounds)

4 medium-size red bell peppers (about 1 pound total
   weight)
1 pound tiny new potatoes
Medium-size white onion
Small red onion
5 large cloves garlic
Small bunch each fresh parsley, basil, and chives, or any
   combination
Small bunch fresh thyme, or ¼ teaspoon dried
5 large eggs
1¾ cups milk
3½ tablespoons unsalted butter, approximately
¾ pound chèvre, such as Montrachet, Bucheron, or Valençay, without rind or ash coating
½ cup plus 2 tablespoons olive oil, approximately
2 tablespoons red wine vinegar
Two 2-ounce tins oil-packed anchovies
⅓ cup plus 1 tablespoon all-purpose flour
Salt
Freshly ground black pepper

UTENSILS

2 medium-size skillets, 1 nonaluminum, 1 with cover
2 medium-size saucepans
Small saucepan
1½-quart soufflé dish
Medium-size bowl, plus additional bowl if using canned
   tomatoes
2 small bowls
Large flat plate or round platter
Salad spinner (optional)
Colander
Strainer
Measuring cups and spoons
Chef's knife
Paring knife
Wooden spoon
Slotted spoon
Whisk
Vegetable brush

START-TO-FINISH STEPS

1. Wash fresh herbs and pat dry with paper towels. Trim
stems from parsley and basil, if using, and discard. Set
aside 4 parsley sprigs for garnish, if using, for soufflé
recipe; mince enough parsley, basil, and/or chives to measure 1½ cups combined for soufflé recipe. Reserve remaining herbs for another use. If using fresh thyme, strip
enough leaves to measure ½ teaspoon for coulis recipe.
Peel 5 cloves garlic; cut 4 cloves into slivers for salad recipe
and mince remaining clove for coulis recipe. Peel red onion
and cut crosswise into ⅛-inch-thick slices for salad recipe.
Peel and coarsely chop white onion for coulis recipe.
2. Follow soufflé recipe steps 1 through 7.
3. While soufflé is baking, follow salad recipe steps 1
through 4.

4. Follow coulis recipe steps 1 through 4.
5. While coulis is cooking, follow salad recipe steps 5
through 12.
6. Follow coulis recipe step 5 and salad recipe step 13, and
serve salad as first course.
7. Follow soufflé recipe step 8 and coulis recipe step 6.
8. Follow soufflé recipe steps 9 and 10, and serve.

RECIPES

Mixed Vegetable and Anchovy Salad

1 pound tiny new potatoes
Two 2-ounce tins oil-packed anchovies
4 medium-size red bell peppers (about 1 pound total
   weight)
6 tablespoons olive oil, approximately
Medium-size head chicory (about 1¼ pounds)
Salt
Freshly ground black pepper
4 large cloves garlic, peeled and cut into slivers
2 tablespoons red wine vinegar
Small red onion, peeled and thinly sliced

1. Bring 1 quart water to a boil in medium-size saucepan
over high heat.
2. While water is heating, scrub potatoes with vegetable
brush and rinse under cold running water.
3. Add potatoes to boiling water and cook about 20 minutes, or until just tender.
4. While potatoes are cooking, turn anchovies into
strainer and rinse under cold running water. Pat dry with
paper towels; set aside.
5. Turn potatoes into colander and cool under cold running
water; drain. Transfer potatoes to small bowl; set aside.
6. Wash peppers and dry with paper towels. Halve, core,
and seed peppers. Cut lengthwise into ¼-inch-wide strips.
7. Heat olive oil in medium-size skillet over medium-high
heat. Add pepper strips and sauté, stirring occasionally,
about 5 minutes, or until tender.
8. While peppers are cooking, wash chicory and dry in
salad spinner or with paper towels. Remove and discard
any bruised or discolored leaves. Divide chicory among 4
salad plates; set aside.
9. Season peppers with salt and pepper to taste and, using
slotted spoon, transfer to plate. Set peppers aside; reserve
oil in skillet.
10. Add garlic to skillet and sauté over medium-high heat
1 minute, or just until golden. With slotted spoon, transfer
garlic to small bowl.
11. With skillet still over medium-high heat, add vinegar
to remaining oil, stirring and scraping up any residue from
bottom of pan. Add salt and pepper to taste and more oil, if
necessary, to measure ¼ cup dressing. Cover pan and
remove from heat.
12. Dry potatoes with paper towels. Cut crosswise into ¼-
inch-thick slices; set aside.
13. Divide onion rings among chicory-lined plates. Top
with equal portions of potatoes, anchovies, and sautéed

peppers. Sprinkle each serving with sautéed garlic, top with warm dressing, and serve.

Herbed Chèvre Soufflé with Tomato Coulis

3½ tablespoons unsalted butter, approximately
⅓ cup plus 1 tablespoon all-purpose flour
¾ pound chèvre, such as Montrachet, Bucheron, or Valençay, without rind or ash coating
5 large eggs
1¾ cups milk
1½ cups combined minced fresh parsley, basil, and chives, or any combination
Salt
Freshly ground black pepper
Tomato Coulis (see following recipe)
4 parsley sprigs for garnish (optional)

1. Preheat oven to 400 degrees.
2. Butter and flour 1½-quart soufflé dish; set aside.
3. Crumble cheese; set aside.
4. Break eggs into medium-size bowl and beat with fork just until combined; set aside.
5. Melt 2½ tablespoons butter in small saucepan over medium heat. Add ⅓ cup flour and cook, stirring, over medium-high heat 1 minute; be careful not to allow mixture to brown.
6. Whisking vigorously, add milk slowly and continue whisking until well blended. Raise heat to high and continue stirring until mixture thickens and begins to boil. Continue to cook another 30 seconds, then remove pan from heat.
7. Add cheese, herbs, and salt and pepper to taste to soufflé base and stir with wooden spoon to combine. Stir in beaten eggs. Pour mixture into prepared dish and bake 40 to 45 minutes, or until puffed and golden.
8. Remove soufflé from oven and set aside to cool 5 minutes.
9. To unmold soufflé, run knife blade around outside to loosen, then place large flat plate or platter over top of soufflé. Holding plate and dish firmly together, turn upside down. Cut soufflé into 8 wedges.
10. Divide tomato coulis among 4 dinner plates, top each serving with 2 wedges of soufflé, and serve garnished with a sprig of parsley, if desired.

Tomato Coulis

¼ cup olive oil
Medium-size white onion, peeled and coarsely chopped
Large clove garlic, peeled and minced
2 medium-size ripe tomatoes (about 1 pound total weight), or 28-ounce can whole tomatoes
½ teaspoon fresh thyme, or ¼ teaspoon dried
Salt
Freshly ground black pepper

1. If using fresh tomatoes, bring 2 quarts water to a boil in medium-size saucepan over high heat.
2. Meanwhile, heat olive oil in medium-size nonaluminum skillet over medium heat. Add onion and garlic, and sauté, stirring occasionally, about 4 minutes, or just until golden and soft.
3. Meanwhile, plunge fresh tomatoes into boiling water for 30 seconds. Turn into colander and refresh under cold water. Remove skins and discard; core, halve, and seed tomatoes; chop coarsely. If using canned tomatoes, turn into strainer set over medium-size bowl. Coarsely chop tomatoes; reserve juice for another use.
4. Add tomatoes and thyme to skillet, season with salt and pepper to taste, and stir to combine. Cook, uncovered, over medium heat 10 to 15 minutes, or until slightly thickened.
5. Taste coulis and adjust seasoning. Cover skillet and set aside.
6. Just before serving, reheat coulis over medium heat for 2 to 3 minutes, or until hot, if desired.

ADDED TOUCH

Inspired by orange *givre*, a popular summertime cooler along the Mediterranean coast, this lemon-lime ice is served in hollowed-out citrus shells.

Lemon-Lime Givre

5 large lemons
5 large limes
¾ cup sugar
1 egg white

1. Wash lemons and limes and dry with paper towels. Using zester or grater, remove enough rind from 1 lemon and 1 lime to measure ½ teaspoon each; set aside.
2. Halve lemons and limes crosswise and squeeze enough juice to measure 1½ cups combined. Place juice in nonaluminum container, cover, and refrigerate.
3. Carefully remove pulp from 4 lemon halves and 4 lime halves; discard pulp. Cut thin slice from rounded bottom of each shell so that it will not roll. Place on plate, cover with plastic wrap, and refrigerate until ready to serve.
4. Combine sugar, grated rind, and ½ cup water in small nonaluminum saucepan and bring to a boil over medium-high heat. Cook, stirring, 2 to 3 minutes, or until sugar is completely dissolved. Remove pan from heat and set aside to cool 15 minutes.
5. Add lemon-lime juice to sugar syrup and stir to combine. Pour mixture into 8-inch metal cake pan and freeze 6 hours.
6. A few hours before serving, beat egg white with electric mixer until stiff; set aside.
7. Break up lemon-lime ice with a fork or cut it into cubes with a knife. Transfer ice to food processor fitted with steel blade and process, pulsing machine on and off a few times, just until lump free. Add beaten egg white and process just until smooth.
8. Divide mixture among lemon and lime shells, mounding slightly, and return to freezer for at least 1 hour.
9. Divide filled lemon and lime shells among 4 dessert plates and serve.

Mary Cleaver

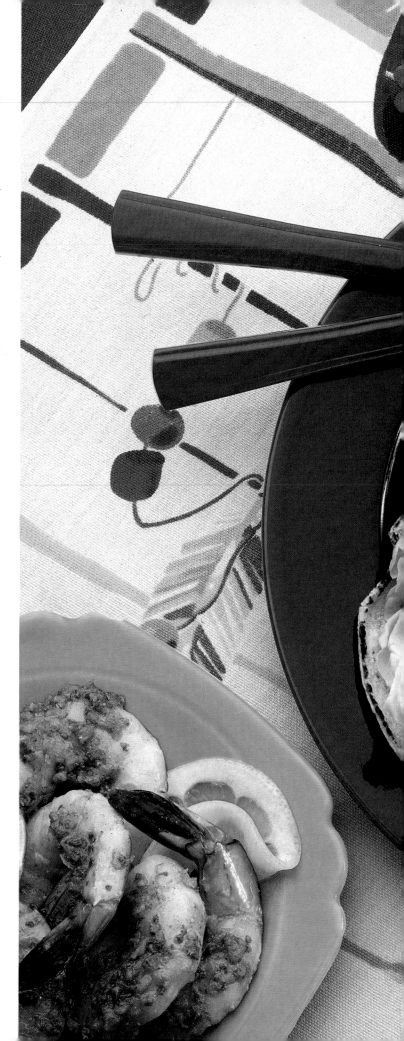

M ary Cleaver strives for diversity when she plans a late meal, often combining recipes from several different cuisines to achieve greater variety in taste and texture. She considers late evening the perfect time for impromptu entertaining and prefers to keep the food simple so she can relax with her guests.

In Menu 1, she fills tortillas with marinated chicken and a Mexican relish made with *poblano* chilies or with bell peppers and sliced *jalapeño*, and supplements this festive combination with shrimp in a Creole-style vinaigrette. The shrimp can be the first course or an accompaniment to the chicken.

Quahogs, the largest variety of hard-shell clam, are featured in Menu 3. The cook stuffs them with a mixture of vegetables and Portuguese *chouriço*, a garlicky smoked sausage similar to Spanish or Mexican *chorizo*. Rather than serve a spicy Latin side dish with the quahogs, she offers maple-flavored cornbread, a New England favorite, because its sweetness offsets the strong flavors in the stuffing.

For the baked-egg main dish of Menu 2, Mary Cleaver uses ingredients likely to be found in most well-stocked kitchens—dried pasta (here *fusilli*), eggs, sweet peppers, olive oil, and assorted seasonings. With the eggs, she serves an unusual salad of grated celery root blended with a mayonnaise flavored with mustard, garlic, and capers.

Tortillas topped with strips of broiled marinated chicken and tomato-chili relish color-complement shrimp in Creole vinaigrette. If you like, serve the tortillas, chicken strips, and relish on separate plates and let your guests create their own meal.

Shrimp with Creole-style Vinaigrette
Broiled Chicken with Tortillas and Tomato-Chili Relish

Corn tortillas, the flat bread of Mexico, are made of *masa harina*, a flour made from dried corn kernels treated with lime. Fresh or frozen corn tortillas can be found in the dairy or frozen food case of most supermarkets and are far superior to the canned type.

WHAT TO DRINK

Serve your guests mugs of cold, thirst-quenching beer with this supper.

SHOPPING LIST AND STAPLES

8 boneless, skinless chicken thighs (about 2 pounds total weight)
1 pound medium-size shrimp, shelled and deveined
1 head Bibb, Boston, or leaf lettuce
6 fresh poblano chilies, or 3 red or green bell peppers
2 medium-size tomatoes (about 1 pound total weight)
Small bunch celery
2 medium-size yellow onions (about 1 pound total weight)
Medium-size red onion
1 bunch Italian parsley
Small bunch coriander
4 cloves garlic
4 limes
8 fresh 7-inch corn tortillas, or 1 package frozen
½ cup olive oil
5 tablespoons vegetable oil
¼ cup sherry wine vinegar
5 tablespoons Creole or Dijon mustard
4-ounce can jalapeño chilies, or 1 fresh jalapeño (if not using poblanos)
1 tablespoon paprika, preferably hot
1 tablespoon ground cumin
2 teaspoons chili powder
1 bay leaf
Salt and freshly ground black pepper
3 peppercorns
2 cups dry white wine

UTENSILS

Food processor (optional)
Medium-size skillet
2 medium-size saucepans, 1 nonaluminum
Broiling pan with rack
Large nonaluminum bowl
Medium-size bowl
Small nonaluminum bowl
Colander
Measuring cups and spoons
Chef's knife
Paring knife
Wooden spoon
Slotted spoon
Long-handled two-pronged fork
Whisk
Metal tongs
Garlic press (optional)
Citrus juicer
Rubber gloves (if using chilies)
Brown paper bag

START-TO-FINISH STEPS

One hour ahead: If using frozen tortillas for chicken recipe, set out to thaw.

1. Wash parsley and coriander, and dry with paper towels. Strip enough parsley leaves to measure ½ cup loosely packed for shrimp recipe. Set aside 4 sprigs of coriander for relish recipe; reserve remainder for another use.
2. Follow shrimp recipe steps 1 through 7.
3. Follow relish recipe step 1 and chicken recipe steps 1 through 6.
4. Follow relish recipe steps 2 through 10.
5. Follow chicken recipe step 7, shrimp recipe step 8, and serve shrimp as first course.
6. Follow chicken recipe steps 8 through 10 and relish recipe step 11.
7. Follow chicken recipe steps 11 and 12, and serve.

RECIPES

Shrimp with Creole-style Vinaigrette

Medium-size red onion
2 stalks celery
½ cup loosely packed parsley leaves
5 tablespoons Creole or Dijon mustard
¼ cup sherry wine vinegar
1 tablespoon paprika, preferably hot
½ cup olive oil
Salt and freshly ground black pepper

2 cups dry white wine
Medium-size yellow onion
3 peppercorns
1 bay leaf
1 pound medium-size shrimp, shelled and deveined

1. Halve and peel red onion. Set one half aside; reserve remaining half for another use. Wash and dry celery. Trim ends and discard. Using food processor or chef's knife, finely mince ½ red onion, celery, and parsley.
2. For vinaigrette, combine minced onion, celery, and parsley with mustard, vinegar, paprika, olive oil, and salt and pepper to taste in small nonaluminum bowl, and whisk until blended. Cover with plastic wrap and refrigerate.
3. Combine wine and 2 cups water in medium-size non-aluminum saucepan and bring to a boil over high heat.
4. While water is heating, halve and peel yellow onion.
5. Add onion, peppercorns, and bay leaf to boiling water. Reduce heat and simmer 5 minutes.
6. Add shrimp to liquid, increase heat to high, and cook just until liquid returns to a boil.
7. Turn shrimp into colander set over large bowl. Refresh shrimp under cold running water; reserve cooking liquid for another use, if desired. Place shrimp in medium-size bowl, cover with plastic wrap, and refrigerate until ready to serve.
8. Whisk vinaigrette to recombine. Divide shrimp among 4 salad plates and top with equal amounts of vinaigrette.

Broiled Chicken with Tortillas and Tomato-Chili Relish

8 boneless, skinless chicken thighs (about 2 pounds)
4 cloves garlic
4 limes
1 tablespoon ground cumin
2 teaspoons chili powder
½ teaspoon salt
1 teaspoon freshly ground black pepper
1 head Bibb, Boston, or leaf lettuce
1 tablespoon vegetable oil
8 fresh 7-inch corn tortillas, or 8 frozen tortillas, thawed
Tomato-Chili Relish (see following recipe)

1. Wash and dry chicken. Cut each thigh lengthwise into 1½-inch-wide strips; set aside.
2. Crush garlic cloves under flat blade of chef's knife; remove and discard peels. Put garlic through press.
3. Squeeze enough lime juice to measure ½ cup.
4. For marinade, combine garlic, lime juice, cumin, chili powder, salt, and pepper in large nonaluminum bowl, and stir with fork until blended.
5. Add chicken to marinade and toss until evenly coated; set aside for at least 15 minutes.
6. Wash and dry lettuce. Remove and discard any bruised or discolored leaves. Wrap in paper towels and refrigerate until ready to serve.
7. Preheat broiler. Remove rack and set pan 4 inches from heating element.

8. Lightly grease broiler rack. Using slotted spoon, transfer chicken to rack and broil 4 minutes.
9. Using metal tongs, turn chicken and broil another 4 minutes, or until juices run clear when chicken is pierced with knife.
10. Meanwhile, stack tortillas and wrap securely in foil; place in oven to warm.
11. Remove tortillas from oven and divide among 4 dinner plates. Top each tortilla with 1 or 2 lettuce leaves.
12. Remove chicken from broiler and divide among lettuce-lined tortillas. Top with tomato-chili relish.

Tomato-Chili Relish

6 fresh poblano chilies, or 3 red or green bell peppers
Medium-size yellow onion
2 medium-size tomatoes (about 1 pound total weight)
4-ounce can jalapeños, or 1 fresh jalapeño (if using bell peppers)
¼ cup vegetable oil
Salt and freshly ground black pepper
4 sprigs coriander

1. Roast chilies or peppers: Spear through top with long-handled two-pronged fork and hold directly over flame of gas burner, or place on foil-lined baking sheet about 4 inches from heating element in broiler, and roast, turning to char skins evenly. Place chilies or peppers in paper bag, close bag securely, and set aside to steam 10 to 20 minutes.
2. In medium-size saucepan, bring 1 quart of water to a boil over high heat.
3. While water is heating, peel onion and cut into ¼-inch-thick slices; set aside.
4. Plunge tomatoes into boiling water for 30 seconds. Turn tomatoes into colander and refresh under cold running water; set aside.
5. Wearing rubber gloves, if using chilies, remove chilies or peppers from bag and, holding each under cold running water, gently rub to remove charred skin; pat dry with paper towels. Halve, core, and seed chilies or peppers. Cut lengthwise into ¼-inch-wide strips; set aside.
6. Wearing rubber gloves, rinse 1 jalapeño, if using, under cold running water and dry with paper towel. Trim stem end, halve lengthwise, and remove seeds with tip of knife. Chop one half; reserve remaining half for another use.
7. Heat oil in medium-size skillet over medium heat. Add onion and sauté, stirring occasionally, 3 to 5 minutes, or just until soft and translucent.
8. Add chili strips, or pepper strips and chopped jalapeño, to onion. Cover pan, reduce heat to low, and cook gently 5 minutes.
9. Meanwhile, peel tomatoes and discard skins. Core, halve, and seed tomatoes; chop coarsely.
10. Add tomatoes to chili or pepper mixture and stir to combine. Add salt and pepper to taste, remove pan from heat, and set aside to cool.
11. Strip coriander leaves from stems; discard stems. Add coriander leaves to relish and stir to combine. Adjust seasoning; set aside until ready to use.

Baked Eggs with Pasta and Peppers
Celery Root Salad

For a casual kitchen dinner, serve the baked-egg main course directly from the skillet, accompanied by celery root salad.

Green *fusilli*, a corkscrew-shaped pasta flavored and colored with spinach, is tossed with basil paste before baking with the eggs and pepper strips. If you cannot find green *fusilli* (also called *rotelle*), use fettuccine or spaghetti, or whatever pasta you prefer. If basil is unavailable, substitute fresh parsley.

WHAT TO DRINK

To complement this colorful late-evening meal, serve a light white wine. A Pinot Grigio or a dry California Chenin Blanc would be ideal.

SHOPPING LIST AND STAPLES

2 medium-size celery roots (about 1½ to 2 pounds
    total weight)
Small head romaine lettuce
3 red bell peppers
1 yellow bell pepper
5 cloves garlic
Large bunch basil or Italian parsley
Small bunch Italian parsley, plus large bunch if not
    using basil
Small bunch fresh chives
2 lemons
9 eggs
1¾ cups olive oil
2 tablespoons Dijon mustard
7-ounce jar cornichons or sour pickles
2-ounce jar capers
¼ pound dried pasta, preferably green fusilli
Salt and freshly ground pepper

UTENSILS

Food processor or blender
Large heavy-gauge ovenproof skillet with cover
Large saucepan
Large nonaluminum bowl
Medium-size bowl
Colander

Small strainer
Measuring cups and spoons
Chef's knife
Paring knife
2 wooden spoons
Rubber spatula
Long-handled two-pronged fork
Metal tongs
Grater (if not using processor)
Brown paper bag

START-TO-FINISH STEPS

1. For baked eggs and salad recipes, crush garlic cloves under flat blade of chef's knife. Remove peels and discard; set garlic aside. Wash parsley, chives, and basil if using, and dry with paper towels. Trim stems from parsley and basil and discard. Mince enough parsley to measure 2 tablespoons each for baked eggs and salad recipes. Strip enough basil or parsley leaves to measure 2 cups, loosely packed, for baked eggs recipe. Snip enough chives to measure 2 tablespoons for baked eggs recipe.
2. Follow baked eggs recipe steps 1 through 11.
3. Follow salad recipe steps 1 through 9 and serve with eggs.

RECIPES

Baked Eggs with Pasta and Peppers

3 red bell peppers
1 yellow bell pepper
Salt
4 cloves garlic, crushed and peeled
2 cups basil or Italian parsley leaves, loosely packed
¾ cup olive oil
¼ pound dried pasta, preferably green fusilli
Freshly ground pepper
8 eggs
2 tablespoons snipped chives
2 tablespoons minced parsley

1. Preheat oven to 350 degrees.
2. Roast peppers: Spear peppers through top with long-handled two-pronged fork and hold directly over flame of gas burner, or place on foil-lined baking sheet about 4 inches from heating element in broiler, and roast, turning to char skins evenly. Place in paper bag, close bag securely, and set aside to steam 10 to 20 minutes.
3. In large saucepan, combine 2 quarts water and 1 tablespoon salt, and bring to a boil over high heat.
4. While water is heating, combine 2 cloves crushed garlic and basil or parsley leaves in food processor fitted with steel blade or in blender, and mince finely.
5. With machine running, add ½ cup olive oil in a slow, steady stream and process until thick and paste-like.
6. Add pasta to boiling water and cook 8 to 10 minutes, or just until *al dente*.

7. While pasta is cooking, combine remaining garlic, ¼ cup olive oil, and salt and pepper to taste in medium-size bowl, and stir with fork to combine; set aside.
8. Remove peppers from bag and, holding each under cold running water, gently rub to remove charred skin; pat dry with paper towels. Halve, core, and seed peppers; cut lengthwise into ½-inch-wide strips. Add strips to bowl with garlic and oil, and toss gently until evenly coated.
9. Turn pasta into colander and run under cold running water to stop the cooking; drain.
10. Transfer pasta to large heavy-gauge ovenproof skillet. Add basil paste and toss to combine.
11. Arrange pepper strips over pasta. Break eggs in circle over peppers. Sprinkle with chives and parsley, and ground pepper to taste. Bake, covered, 20 to 25 minutes, or just until egg whites are set. Serve from skillet in wedges.

Celery Root Salad

2 lemons
2 medium-size celery roots (about 1½ to 2 pounds total weight)
Small head romaine lettuce
½ teaspoon capers
3 cornichons or small sour pickle
1 clove garlic, crushed and peeled
1 egg
2 tablespoons Dijon mustard
1 cup olive oil
2 tablespoons minced parsley
Salt and freshly ground pepper

1. Squeeze enough lemon juice to measure 6 tablespoons.
2. In large nonaluminum bowl, combine ¼ cup lemon juice and 3 cups cold water; set aside.
3. Trim and peel celery roots. If using food processor, fit with shredding disk. Cut celery roots into pieces that will fit in feed tube, and shred. Or, shred on coarse side of grater. Place shredded celery root in bowl with lemon water; set aside. Rinse processor bowl, if using.
4. Wash and dry lettuce. Remove and discard any bruised or discolored leaves. Line platter with lettuce.
5. Place capers in small strainer and rinse under cold running water; set aside to drain. Coarsely chop enough cornichons or pickle to measure 1 tablespoon.
6. For dressing, combine capers, chopped cornichons or pickle, garlic, egg, remaining 2 tablespoons lemon juice, and mustard in processor or blender, and process 10 seconds, or just until combined.
7. With machine running, add oil drop by drop until mixture binds up and thickens, then add remaining oil in a slow, steady stream and process until oil has been totally incorporated and mixture is thick and smooth.
8. Add parsley, and salt and pepper to taste, and process just until combined; set aside.
9. Drain celery root. Add dressing, one half at a time, tossing after each addition to combine. Turn salad out onto lettuce-lined platter and serve.

Stuffed Quahogs
Tossed Salad
Maple Cornbread

Stuffed quahogs, capped with their own shells, are an unexpected and delicious late-night supper served with a tart mixed salad. Wedges of maple-flavored cornbread add a touch of sweetness to the meal.

When purchasing quahogs, avoid any that have cracked shells or that do not close when you tap their shells. As a substitute, use 24 large-capped mushrooms with the stems removed (allowing 6 per person), and add 2 cups of minced clams to the stuffing mixture.

WHAT TO DRINK

For this menu, choose a full-bodied white wine, such as a California Sauvignon Blanc or Chardonnay.

SHOPPING LIST AND STAPLES

24 quahogs (about 10 pounds total weight)
1 pound Portuguese chouriço or other spicy sausage
1 head each red leaf and Boston lettuce
Medium-size green bell pepper
Small carrot
Medium-size yellow onion
4 cloves garlic
1 bunch Italian parsley
Small bunch fresh sage, or 1 teaspoon dried
1 egg
1½ cups milk
1 pint heavy cream
½ cup plus 2 tablespoons olive oil
¼ cup corn oil
¼ cup balsamic vinegar or red wine vinegar
1 heaping teaspoon Dijon mustard
⅓ cup maple syrup
1 cup yellow or white cornmeal
½ cup all-purpose flour
½ cup whole-wheat flour
¼ cup dry bread crumbs
2 teaspoons baking powder
Cayenne pepper
Salt and freshly ground pepper

UTENSILS

Food processor (optional)
Stockpot or deep kettle with cover
Medium-size skillet with cover
10-inch cast-iron skillet with ovenproof handle
13 x 9 x 2-inch baking dish
2 large bowls
2 medium-size bowls
Small jar with tight-fitting lid

Colander
Measuring cups and spoons
Chef's knife
Paring knife
2 wooden spoons
Metal spatula
Rubber spatula
Grater (if not using processor)

START-TO-FINISH STEPS

1. Crush and peel garlic.
2. Follow cornbread recipe steps 1 through 5.
3. While cornbread is baking, follow quahogs recipe steps 1 through 15.
4. While quahogs and cornbread are baking, follow salad recipe steps 1 through 5.
5. Follow quahogs recipe step 16 and cornbread recipe step 6, and serve with salad.

RECIPES

Stuffed Quahogs

24 quahogs (about 10 pounds total weight)
1 bunch Italian parsley
Medium-size green bell pepper
Medium-size yellow onion
3 cloves garlic, crushed and peeled
2 tablespoons olive oil
1 pound Portuguese chouriço or other spicy sausage
¼ cup dry bread crumbs
Pinch of Cayenne pepper
Salt and freshly ground pepper

1. Fill stockpot or kettle with about 2 inches of water, cover, and bring to a boil over high heat.
2. Meanwhile, scrub and rinse quahogs. Add quahogs to boiling water, cover pot, and return to a boil. Cook quahogs 5 to 8 minutes, or until they are open wide.
3. Wash and dry parsley. Strip enough leaves from stems to measure 1 cup, loosely packed, and set aside.
4. Wash and dry bell pepper. Halve, core, and seed pepper. Cut each half into quarters; set aside.
5. Turn quahogs into colander; remove and discard any unopened quahogs. Set remaining quahogs aside to cool.
6. Peel and quarter onion; set aside.
7. Dice bell pepper, onion, and garlic in food processor, or dice with chef's knife.
8. Heat olive oil in medium-size skillet over low heat. Add vegetables and cook, covered, about 3 minutes, or until soft but not brown. Rinse and dry processor bowl.
9. Meanwhile, remove sausage from casing and dice finely in food processor or with chef's knife.
10. Remove cover from skillet and raise heat to medium. Add sausage and cook, stirring occasionally, another 3 minutes.
11. Remove skillet from heat and set aside to cool slightly.
12. Remove meat from all the quahogs, reserving 12 whole shells, and finely chop meat in processor or with chef's knife; transfer to medium-size bowl.
13. Finely chop parsley; add to quahog mixture.
14. Add bread crumbs, vegetable-sausage mixture, Cayenne, and salt and pepper to taste to quahog mixture, and stir to combine.
15. Break 12 reserved shells in half and rinse and dry, if necessary. Generously pack bottom halves with stuffing and partially cover with top shells. Place in large ovenproof baking dish and bake on top rack of preheated 350-degree oven 10 to 15 minutes, or until heated through.
16. Remove quahogs from oven and divide among 4 dinner plates.

Tossed Salad

Small bunch fresh sage, or 1 teaspoon dried
1 clove garlic, crushed and peeled
1 heaping teaspoon Dijon mustard
¼ cup balsamic vinegar or red wine vinegar
½ cup olive oil
Salt and freshly ground pepper
1 head each red leaf and Boston lettuce
Small carrot

1. Rinse fresh sage, if using, and dry with paper towels. Finely chop enough to measure 2 teaspoons.
2. Combine garlic, mustard, vinegar, olive oil, and salt and pepper to taste in small jar with lid and shake until blended. Taste and adjust seasoning; set aside.
3. Wash and dry lettuce. Tear lettuce into bite-size pieces and place in large bowl.
4. Peel carrot. Cut into ¼-inch julienne; add to lettuce.
5. Shake dressing to recombine. Discard garlic clove. Pour dressing over salad and toss until evenly coated.

Maple Cornbread

1 cup yellow or white cornmeal
½ cup whole-wheat flour
½ cup all-purpose flour
2 teaspoons baking powder
1 egg
¼ cup corn oil
⅓ cup maple syrup
1½ cups heavy cream
1½ cups milk

1. Preheat oven to 350 degrees.
2. Grease 10-inch cast-iron skillet with ovenproof handle.
3. Combine dry ingredients in medium-size bowl and stir with fork to blend.
4. Using your fist, make a well in center. Add remaining ingredients in order as listed and stir, gradually incorporating ingredients, until well blended.
5. Pour batter into prepared pan and bake 45 minutes, or until top is golden and sides of bread pull away from pan. The top will be spongy.
6. Remove cornbread from oven and cut into wedges. Divide among 4 small plates and serve.

Sarah Belk Rian

MENU 1 (Left)
Chilled Tomato-Basil Soup
Saffron Risotto with Peppers and Chorizo
Citrus and Fennel Salad

MENU 2
Cream of Potato Soup with Crème Fraîche
and Caviar
Pork Scallops with White Wine and Caraway
Braised Red Cabbage

MENU 3
Chicken with Balsamic Vinegar Sauce
and Prosciutto
Herbed Pasta
Sautéed Arugula with Radicchio

If Sarah Belk Rian were asked to pick one cuisine that has shaped her cooking style more than any other, without hesitation she would say it is Italian. "A trip to Rome when I was an art student permanently changed my views on food," she says. "I loved the unpretentious quality of Italian cooking." Her Menus 1 and 3 consist of lightly seasoned Italian dishes that are appropriate for late-night eating.

Menu 1 begins with a well-chilled tomato soup seasoned with garlic and basil and followed by this cook's version of the popular Italian rice dish *risotto*. Unlike its classic (and time-consuming) counterpart, this recipe requires only occasional stirring and minimal attention while simmering. It also keeps for a short time after cooking without becoming glutinous and gummy—an advantage when it is served as a second course.

In Menu 3, balsamic vinegar and prosciutto—two Italian favorites—flavor the chicken breasts. With the chicken the cook presents arugula, sautéed with garlic, salt, olive oil, and lemon juice, on a bed of radicchio, and a side dish of pasta with fresh herbs.

Sarah Rian is also a great believer in cooking ahead of time for parties—particularly when the event is scheduled for late in the evening. For Menu 2, you can prepare the potato soup recipe in the morning, reheat it when ready to serve, and then add the *crème fraîche* and caviar. And to save even more time, shred the cabbage leaves ahead of time, then wrap them in a plastic bag and refrigerate them. The pork scallops cook quickly and can be prepared at the last minute.

Chilled tomato soup garnished with basil precedes the saffron-tinted risotto, flavored and textured with spicy chorizo sausage, peas, onions, and sweet peppers. A light salad of fresh fennel and citrus fruits is an appealing accompaniment.

45

Chilled Tomato-Basil Soup
Saffron Risotto with Peppers and Chorizo
Citrus and Fennel Salad

To make *risotto* in the traditional way, use Italian Arborio rice, a plump, short-grain variety grown in northern Italy, which becomes creamy when cooked. Look for it in Italian groceries, specialty food shops, and some supermarkets. Highly seasoned *chorizo* sausage, used in Mexican and Spanish cooking, adds zest to the rice dish. Made from coarsely ground pork, *chorizo* is sold in bulk or links at butcher shops and ethnic markets.

WHAT TO DRINK

With this Italian meal, try a young red wine with a lot of fruit, such as a California Zinfandel, an Italian Chianti, or a Spanish Rioja.

SHOPPING LIST AND STAPLES

½ pound chorizo
2 fennel bulbs (1½ to 2 pounds total weight), or small bunch celery and ½ teaspoon fennel seeds
Small green bell pepper
Small red bell pepper
1 head Boston lettuce
Small Spanish onion
Small yellow onion
3 medium-size cloves garlic
Small bunch fresh basil, or 1 tablespoon dried
2 medium-size oranges
Medium-size pink grapefruit
3 tablespoons unsalted butter
10-ounce package frozen peas
1 quart chicken stock, preferably homemade (see page 8), or canned
16-ounce can Italian plum tomatoes
18-ounce can tomato juice
6 tablespoons virgin olive oil
2 tablespoons red wine vinegar
1½ cups Arborio rice (¾ pound)
1 teaspoon saffron threads
Salt and freshly ground black pepper
½ cup dry white vermouth

UTENSILS

Food processor or blender
Medium-size skillet
Medium-size heavy-gauge saucepan
3-quart ovenproof serving dish
2 large bowls, 1 nonaluminum
Small bowl
Measuring cups and spoons
Chef's knife
Paring knife
2 wooden spoons
Slotted spoon

START-TO-FINISH STEPS

One hour ahead: With large, heavy knife or cleaver, cut through package of frozen peas, dividing the package into one-third and two-third portions. Place the larger portion in plastic bag and return to freezer for another use. Place smaller portion in small bowl and set aside to thaw.

1. Peel and mince 3 cloves garlic for soup, risotto, and salad recipes.
2. Follow soup recipe steps 1 through 4.
3. Follow salad recipe steps 1 through 4.
4. Follow risotto recipe steps 1 through 10.
5. Follow soup recipe step 5 and serve as first course.
6. Follow salad recipe steps 5 and 6, and serve with risotto.

RECIPES

Chilled Tomato-Basil Soup

Small Spanish onion
Small bunch fresh basil, or 1 tablespoon dried
1 teaspoon minced garlic
16-ounce can Italian plum tomatoes
2 cups tomato juice
3 tablespoons virgin olive oil
1 tablespoon red wine vinegar
Salt and freshly ground black pepper
6 ice cubes

1. Peel onion and coarsely chop enough to measure ½ cup.
2. Wash fresh basil, if using, and dry with paper towels. Trim stems and discard; set aside 1 sprig for garnish, if desired. Finely chop enough basil to measure 3 table-spoons; reserve remainder for another use.
3. Combine onion, chopped or dried basil, garlic, plum tomatoes with their juice, ½ cup tomato juice, olive oil, vinegar, and salt and pepper to taste in blender or, work-ing in batches, in food processor, and process until smooth.

4. Turn mixture into large nonaluminum bowl. Stir in remaining tomato juice and ice cubes. Adjust seasoning, cover, and refrigerate until ready to serve.

5. When ready to serve, remove and discard any unmelted pieces of ice. Turn soup into tureen or large bowl and garnish with a sprig of basil, if desired.

Saffron Risotto with Peppers and Chorizo

1 quart chicken stock
½ cup dry white vermouth
1 teaspoon saffron threads
Small yellow onion
Small green bell pepper
Small red bell pepper
1½ cups Arborio rice
½ pound chorizo
3 tablespoons unsalted butter
½ cup frozen peas, thawed
1 tablespoon minced garlic

1. Preheat oven to 200 degrees.

2. Combine stock, vermouth, and saffron in medium-size heavy-gauge saucepan and bring to a boil over high heat.

3. While mixture is coming to a boil, peel and finely chop onion; you should have about ½ cup. Wash peppers and dry with paper towels. Halve, core, and seed peppers. Cut into ½-inch dice; you should have about ½ cup each. Set aside.

4. Add rice to boiling liquid, reduce heat to medium, and simmer gently, uncovered, stirring occasionally, 25 to 30 minutes, or until rice is tender and only about 1 tablespoon of liquid remains on top of rice. Do not stir too often or rice will be gummy.

5. While rice simmers, cut chorizo crosswise into ¼-inch-thick slices.

6. Melt 2 tablespoons butter in medium-size skillet over medium heat. Add onion and peppers, and sauté, stirring frequently, 5 minutes, or until soft. Using slotted spoon, transfer onion and peppers to ovenproof serving dish.

7. Add chorizo to skillet and sauté over medium heat, stirring frequently, 3 to 5 minutes, or until slices begin to brown and crisp slightly. Using slotted spoon, transfer chorizo to dish with onion and peppers.

8. Add remaining 1 tablespoon butter to skillet. When butter stops foaming, add peas and cook 2 to 3 minutes, or just until heated through. Remove pan from heat.

9. Off heat, add garlic to skillet and stir 1 minute, or just until garlic releases its fragrance. Add pea mixture to chorizo.

10. When rice is done, add to chorizo mixture and toss gently to combine. Cover dish tightly with foil and keep warm in oven until ready to serve.

Citrus and Fennel Salad

3 tablespoons virgin olive oil
1 tablespoon red wine vinegar
½ teaspoon minced garlic
Pinch of salt
Freshly ground black pepper
2 fennel bulbs (1½ to 2 pounds total weight), or 5 stalks celery and ½ teaspoon crushed fennel seeds
2 medium-size oranges
Medium-size pink grapefruit
1 head Boston lettuce

1. In small bowl, combine oil, vinegar, garlic, salt, pepper to taste, and crushed fennel seeds, if using, and beat with fork until blended; set aside.

2. Wash fennel or celery and dry with paper towels. Trim ends, reserving feathery fennel tops for garnish. If using fennel, cut stalks and bulbs crosswise into ½-inch-wide pieces; then halve large pieces of bulbs crosswise to make pieces of uniform size. You will have 2½ to 3 cups. If using celery, cut crosswise into ½-inch-wide pieces. Place fennel or celery in large bowl; set aside.

3. Using sharp paring knife, peel oranges and grapefruit, removing as much white pith as possible; discard peel. Working over the large bowl, segment fruits, then cut orange sections in half and grapefruit sections into thirds, if large. Cover with plastic wrap and refrigerate until ready to serve.

4. Wash lettuce and dry with paper towels. Remove and discard any bruised or discolored leaves. Wrap lettuce in paper towels and refrigerate until ready to serve.

5. When ready to serve, line serving platter with lettuce.

6. Stir dressing to recombine. Pour dressing over salad and toss until evenly coated. Turn out onto lettuce-lined platter and serve garnished with fennel tops, if desired.

ADDED TOUCH

This unusual ice cream sauce is made by simmering cut-up dried figs in Marsala, a fortified Italian wine.

Figs Marsala with Ice Cream

1 lemon
¾ cup Marsala
¼ cup sugar
8 dried figs (about 6 ounces total weight)
1 pint vanilla ice cream

1. Wash and dry lemon. Halve lemon crosswise. Slice one half thinly; reserve remaining half for another use.

2. Combine lemon slices, Marsala, and sugar in small nonaluminum saucepan and bring to a simmer over medium heat.

3. While liquid is coming to a simmer, trim stems from figs and cut figs into ½-inch dice; you will have about 1 cup. Add figs to liquid and simmer, uncovered, 10 minutes.

4. With slotted spoon, transfer figs to small bowl. Raise heat to high and bring poaching liquid to a boil. Continue boiling about 10 minutes, or until liquid is syrupy and reduced to about ⅓ cup.

5. With slotted spoon, remove lemon slices and discard. Pour reduced poaching liquid through sieve held over figs.

6. Divide ice cream among 4 dessert glasses or bowls. Top each serving with figs and syrup, and serve.

Cream of Potato Soup with Crème Fraîche and Caviar
Pork Scallops with White Wine and Caraway
Braised Red Cabbage

Jazzy tableware and bright flowers complement this supper of creamy potato soup, pork scallops, and wine-braised red cabbage.

The elegant garnish of *crème fraîche* and caviar transforms this simple potato soup into a very special first course. When choosing caviar, let your budget guide you; any type, from inexpensive lumpfish to costly Russian sevruga, will complement this soup. For more information on caviar, see page 9. If you are not a caviar fancier, use minced chives or scallions, or *crème fraîche* alone. For a lighter soup, add half-and-half or milk instead of heavy cream, and omit the *crème fraîche*.

WHAT TO DRINK

A Riesling from California or Germany would be the perfect choice for this menu. Or, consider Champagne, especially if you are splurging on top-quality caviar.

SHOPPING LIST AND STAPLES

Eight ½-inch-thick pork tenderloin scallops, pounded to ¼-inch thickness (about 1½ pounds total weight)
4 or 5 medium-size boiling potatoes (about 1¾ pounds total weight)
Small head red cabbage (about 1 pound)
Large yellow onion
Small bunch celery
Small bunch parsley (optional)
1¼ cups chicken stock, preferably homemade (see page 8), or canned
1 stick plus 6 tablespoons unsalted butter
½ pint heavy cream
¼ cup crème fraîche, or 8-ounce container sour cream
2-ounce jar caviar
5 tablespoons all-purpose flour
1½ teaspoons granulated sugar
2 teaspoons caraway seeds
Salt and freshly ground white pepper
½ cup dry white wine
⅓ cup dry red wine
⅓ cup Madeira

UTENSILS

Food processor or blender
Large skillet with cover
Large sauté pan with cover
Large nonaluminum saucepan with cover
2 medium-size saucepans
Ovenproof platter
Large ovenproof bowl
2 small bowls
Colander
Measuring cups and spoons
Chef's knife
Paring knife
Wooden spoon
Rubber spatula

Wire whisk
Metal tongs
Vegetable peeler
Ladle

START-TO-FINISH STEPS

1. Follow soup recipe steps 1 through 10.
2. Follow cabbage recipe steps 1 through 3.
3. While cabbage is cooking, follow pork recipe steps 1 through 7.
4. Follow cabbage recipe step 4.
5. Follow soup recipe steps 11 through 13 and serve as first course.
6. Follow pork recipe steps 8 through 12 and serve with cabbage.

RECIPES

Cream of Potato Soup with Crème Fraîche and Caviar

Salt
4 or 5 medium-size boiling potatoes (about 1¾ pounds)
Large yellow onion
2 stalks celery
4 tablespoons unsalted butter
1¼ cups chicken stock
1 cup heavy cream
Pinch of freshly ground white pepper
¼ cup crème fraîche or sour cream
4 teaspoons caviar

1. Bring 1½ quarts lightly salted water to a boil in each of 2 medium-size saucepans over medium-high heat.
2. While water is heating, peel potatoes. Cut enough potatoes into ½-inch dice to measure 2 cups; cut remaining potatoes into quarters.
3. Add diced potatoes to one saucepan of boiling water and quartered potatoes to the other. Cook, uncovered, over medium-high heat, 10 to 15 minutes for diced potatoes and 20 minutes for quartered potatoes, or until tender when pierced with tip of knife.
4. While potatoes are cooking, halve and peel onion. Finely chop enough to measure about 1½ cups; set aside.
5. Wash celery and dry with paper towels. Trim ends and discard. Finely chop celery.
6. Heat butter in large nonaluminum saucepan over medium heat. Add onion and celery, and sauté, stirring occasionally, about 10 minutes, or until very tender.
7. Transfer onion and celery to food processor or blender and process about 1 minute, or until puréed. Return purée to saucepan.
8. Drain diced potatoes and add to onion-celery purée.
9. Drain quartered potatoes and transfer to food processor or blender. Add stock and process until puréed.
10. Add potato purée, heavy cream, pepper, and salt to taste to saucepan with diced potatoes and stir to combine.

Cover pan and set aside until ready to serve.

11. Just before serving, reheat soup over medium-high heat until steaming; do *not* boil.

12. While soup is heating, turn crème fraîche or sour cream into small bowl. Using rubber spatula, gently fold in caviar, taking care not to break the delicate eggs.

13. Remove soup from heat. Ladle hot soup and diced potatoes into 4 bowls, top each serving with spoonful of caviar mixture, and serve immediately.

Pork Scallops with White Wine and Caraway

5 tablespoons all-purpose flour
½ teaspoon salt
Eight ½-inch-thick pork tenderloin scallops, pounded to ¼-inch thickness (about 1½ pounds total weight)
6 tablespoons unsalted butter
½ cup dry white wine
2 teaspoons caraway seeds
Small bunch parsley for garnish (optional)

1. Preheat oven to 200 degrees.

2. Place 3 tablespoons flour on large sheet of waxed paper. Add ¼ teaspoon salt and stir to combine; set aside.

3. Rinse scallops under cold running water and dry with paper towels; set aside.

4. In large skillet, heat 2 tablespoons butter over medium heat.

5. Meanwhile, working quickly, dust as many scallops with flour mixture as will fit comfortably in skillet without crowding. Gently shake off excess flour and add scallops to skillet. Cook, uncovered, 3 to 5 minutes per side, or until golden brown.

6. Using metal tongs, transfer scallops to ovenproof platter, cover loosely with foil, and keep warm in oven until ready to serve. Add another 2 tablespoons butter to skillet and repeat process for remaining scallops.

7. For sauce, add wine, ¼ cup water, and caraway seeds to skillet and bring to a rapid boil, scraping up any brown bits clinging to bottom of pan. Cover, remove from heat, and set aside.

8. Return sauce to a boil over medium-high heat. Continue boiling 5 to 10 minutes, or until sauce is reduced to ⅓ cup.

9. Meanwhile, rinse parsley, if using, and dry with paper towels. Trim stems and discard. Mince enough parsley to measure 1 tablespoon; reserve remainder for another use.

10. Combine remaining 2 tablespoons butter with remaining 2 tablespoons flour in small bowl. Using back of spoon, blend into a paste.

11. Remove sauce from heat. Whisk in just enough flour paste to thicken sauce lightly; it should just coat the back of a wooden spoon.

12. Divide scallops among 4 dinner plates, top with sauce, and sprinkle with chopped parsley, if desired.

Braised Red Cabbage

Small head red cabbage (about 1 pound)
4 tablespoons unsalted butter

⅓ cup dry red wine
⅓ cup Madeira
1½ teaspoons granulated sugar
½ teaspoon salt

1. Remove and discard any bruised or discolored outer leaves from cabbage. Quarter cabbage lengthwise; remove and discard core. Using food processor fitted with shredding disk, or chef's knife, cut cabbage into very thin shreds; you will have about 4 cups.

2. Heat butter in large sauté pan over medium heat. Add cabbage and cook, tossing occasionally, 5 minutes, or until cabbage begins to soften.

3. Stir in remaining ingredients, cover, and cook over medium-low heat, stirring occasionally, 15 to 20 minutes, or until cabbage is tender and all but a few tablespoons of the braising liquid has been absorbed.

4. Transfer cabbage to ovenproof bowl, cover loosely with foil, and keep warm in 200-degree oven until ready to serve.

ADDED TOUCH

If you have them, use the traditional lidded porcelain pots for this classic French dessert.

Bittersweet Pots de Crème

4 ounces bittersweet chocolate
Small orange
6 tablespoons milk
1 egg
1 egg yolk
1 tablespoon granulated sugar
1½ teaspoons orange liqueur
½ cup heavy cream (optional)
4 pieces candied orange peel (optional)

1. Using a chef's knife, chop chocolate; set aside.

2. Wash orange and dry with paper towel. With zester or grater, remove enough rind, avoiding white pith as much as possible, to measure 1½ teaspoons; reserve remainder of orange for another use.

3. In small nonaluminum saucepan, scald milk over medium-low heat.

4. Meanwhile, combine chocolate, zest, whole egg, egg yolk, sugar, and liqueur in food processor or blender, and process until well blended.

5. With machine running, add scalded milk to chocolate mixture in a slow, steady stream and process until well blended.

6. Divide mixture among 4 pots de crème, demitasse cups, or individual soufflé dishes. Cover with plastic wrap and chill about 2 hours, or until set.

7. If using cream, one-half hour before serving, place bowl and beaters in freezer to chill.

8. Just before serving, pour cream into chilled bowl and beat with electric mixer until stiff.

9. Top each dessert with whipped cream and serve garnished with a piece of candied orange peel, if desired.

Chicken with Balsamic Vinegar Sauce and Prosciutto
Herbed Pasta
Sautéed Arugula with Radicchio

For an Italian late-night supper, serve chicken breasts with prosciutto, radicchio and arugula salad, and herbed pasta.

Prosciutto and balsamic vinegar provide a distinctive salty-sweet accent for the chicken breasts. Prosciutto is a rather salty air-cured ham prized for its delicate flavor. It should be deep pink in color and appetizingly moist, and should be thinly sliced. Black Forest, Westphalian, or Smithfield ham can be used in this recipe instead of the prosciutto.

Because balsamic vinegar is well aged and therefore mellower than regular wine vinegar, its full, rich flavor makes a good foundation for the *beurre blanc*-style sauce. If you finish preparing the sauce and dinner is delayed for some reason, store the sauce in an insulated vacuum bottle until serving time.

A light salad of two unusual leaf vegetables accompanies the chicken. Arugula is an Italian salad green with narrow frilled leaves and a distinctive peppery taste, rather like that of watercress. Before using, rinse arugula thoroughly to remove any sand, then drain it and gently pat it dry. Radicchio, a ruby-red Italian chicory, has cup-shaped leaves and a pleasantly bitter taste. Traditionally considered a winter vegetable, radicchio is now sold year round at quality greengroceries and well-stocked supermarkets. If neither radicchio nor arugula is available, substitute watercress.

WHAT TO DRINK

With the chicken and prosciutto, serve either a light- to medium-bodied red wine or a full-bodied white. For red, try a California Merlot or an Italian Gattinara or Ghemme; for white, California Chardonnay or French Burgundy would be excellent.

SHOPPING LIST AND STAPLES

4 whole boneless, skinless chicken breasts, halved (about 1½ pounds total weight)
¼ pound thinly sliced prosciutto
2 to 3 bunches arugula (about ¾ pound total weight)
Small head radicchio (about ¼ pound)
Large shallot
3 large cloves garlic
Small bunch fresh thyme or oregano (if available), or ½ teaspoon dried
Small bunch fresh chives (optional)
Small bunch parsley
1 lemon
2 sticks unsalted butter, approximately
½ pint heavy cream
¼ cup virgin olive oil
1 tablespoon vegetable oil
¼ cup balsamic vinegar
½ pound dried capellini or angel hair pasta
Salt
Freshly ground pepper
¼ cup dry red wine

UTENSILS

Nonaluminum stockpot with cover
Large nonaluminum skillet
Medium-size sauté pan or skillet
Small nonaluminum saucepan
Ovenproof platter
Medium-size ovenproof bowl
Small bowl or plate
Colander
Measuring cups and spoons
Chef's knife
Paring knife
Wooden spoon
Slotted spoon
Slotted metal spatula
Small wire whisk
Metal tongs

START-TO-FINISH STEPS

1. Follow arugula and radicchio recipe steps 1 through 6.
2. Follow chicken recipe steps 1 through 7.
3. While chicken is sautéing, follow pasta recipe step 1 and arugula and radicchio recipe steps 7 and 8.
4. Follow chicken recipe step 8 and pasta recipe step 2.
5. Follow chicken recipe step 9 and pasta recipe steps 3 and 4.
6. Follow chicken recipe step 10 and pasta recipe steps 5 and 6.
7. Follow arugula and radicchio recipe step 9, chicken recipe steps 11 through 14, and serve with pasta.

RECIPES

Chicken with Balsamic Vinegar Sauce and Prosciutto

4 whole boneless, skinless chicken breasts, halved (about 1½ pounds total weight)
Large shallot
1 stick plus 4 tablespoons unsalted butter
¼ pound thinly sliced prosciutto
¼ cup balsamic vinegar
¼ cup dry red wine
Salt and freshly ground pepper

1. Preheat oven to 200 degrees.
2. Rinse chicken breasts under cold running water and dry with paper towels; set aside.
3. Peel and finely chop shallot.
4. Heat 2 tablespoons butter in large nonaluminum skillet over medium heat. Add shallot and sauté, stirring occasionally, 3 to 4 minutes, or until softened.
5. While shallot is sautéing, stack slices of prosciutto and cut into ¼-inch-wide strips.
6. Add prosciutto to skillet and sauté, stirring, another minute. Turn shallot-prosciutto mixture into small bowl or onto plate and set aside.

7. Return skillet to medium heat and add 2 tablespoons butter. When butter is hot, add chicken breasts and cook very gently, uncovered, over medium-low heat, 6 to 8 minutes on one side, regulating temperature to avoid burning butter.

8. Using metal tongs, turn breasts and cook another 6 to 8 minutes on other side, or just until juices run clear when breasts are pierced in thickest part.

9. With slotted metal spatula, transfer chicken to ovenproof platter, cover loosely with foil, and keep warm in oven. Pour off fat and set skillet aside.

10. For sauce, return skillet to medium-high heat, add vinegar and wine, and bring to a boil, uncovered, scraping up any brown bits clinging to bottom of skillet. Continue boiling 3 to 4 minutes, or until mixture is reduced to about 1½ tablespoons.

11. Remove skillet from heat and set aside 1 minute to cool.

12. Meanwhile, cut remaining stick of butter into 1-tablespoon pieces.

13. Off heat, add butter to skillet, 1 tablespoon at a time, whisking after each addition until totally incorporated. Add salt and pepper to taste, taking care not to oversalt.

14. Divide chicken among 4 dinner plates, spoon sauce around chicken, and top with prosciutto mixture.

Herbed Pasta

Salt
1 tablespoon vegetable oil
Small bunch parsley
Small bunch fresh thyme or oregano (if available),
    or ½ teaspoon dried
Small bunch fresh chives (optional)
½ pound dried capellini or angel hair pasta
½ cup heavy cream
3 tablespoons unsalted butter

1. Combine 4 quarts water, 1 tablespoon salt, and vegetable oil in nonaluminum stockpot and bring to a boil over high heat.

2. Wash herbs and dry with paper towels. Trim stems from parsley and discard. If using thyme or oregano, mince enough leaves to measure 1 teaspoon. If using chives, mince enough to measure 1 teaspoon. Mince enough parsley to measure 1½ tablespoons if using other fresh herbs; if not, mince enough to measure 3 tablespoons.

3. Add pasta to boiling water, stir to separate strands, and cook 7 to 10 minutes, or according to package directions.

4. Meanwhile, combine cream, butter, herbs, and ¼ teaspoon salt in small nonaluminum saucepan and heat over medium-low heat, stirring once or twice, until hot.

5. Turn pasta into colander and drain.

6. Pour sauce into stockpot, add pasta, and toss gently to combine. Cover and keep warm until ready to serve.

Sautéed Arugula with Radicchio

Small head radicchio (about ¼ pound)
2 to 3 bunches arugula (about ¾ pound total weight)
3 large cloves garlic
¼ cup virgin olive oil
1 lemon
Pinch of salt

1. Remove and discard any bruised or discolored outer leaves from radicchio. Separate leaves; cut out core and discard. Wash leaves and dry with paper towels. Set aside 8 leaves; reserve remainder for another use.

2. Wash arugula and dry with paper towels. Trim stems and discard. Set arugula aside.

3. Peel garlic and cut into slivers; set aside.

4. Heat oil in medium-size sauté pan or skillet over medium heat. Add garlic and sauté, stirring occasionally, 3 to 5 minutes, or until garlic releases its fragrance and has turned golden but not brown.

5. Meanwhile, halve lemon and squeeze enough juice from one half to measure 1 teaspoon. Reserve remaining half for another use.

6. With slotted spoon, remove garlic from pan and discard; set pan aside.

7. Return pan to medium heat, add arugula to pan, and cook, uncovered, over medium-low heat, stirring frequently, about 2 minutes, or until leaves are wilted.

8. Add lemon juice and salt to arugula and toss to combine. Turn into medium-size ovenproof bowl, cover loosely with foil, and keep warm in preheated 200-degree oven until ready to serve.

9. When ready to serve, arrange 2 radicchio leaves, overlapping slightly, on each of 4 dinner plates and top radicchio with equal portions of arugula.

ADDED TOUCH

If macadamias are unavailable, you can use blanched almonds or hazelnuts, but they must be briefly toasted first: Place the nuts in a single layer on a baking sheet and toast in a preheated 300-degree oven 10 to 12 minutes, or until lightly browned. Shake the pan occasionally to prevent scorching. Allow the nuts to cool before adding them to the chocolate.

Chocolate-Nut Clusters

8 ounces milk chocolate or semisweet chocolate
1 tablespoon vegetable oil
1 cup macadamia nuts or whole blanched almonds

1. Bring 1 quart of water to a simmer in bottom of double boiler over medium-low heat.

2. Combine chocolate and vegetable oil in top of double boiler and place over, not in, barely simmering water for 10 minutes, or until chocolate is melted.

3. Meanwhile, line cookie sheet with waxed paper.

4. When chocolate is melted, remove from heat and stir in nuts.

5. Drop chocolate-nut mixture by tablespoonsful onto waxed-paper-lined cookie sheet and refrigerate about 2 hours, or until very firm.

David Kimmel and Steven Petusevsky

B oth David Kimmel and Steven Petusevsky feel that late-night suppers are a time to be innovative. They like to use exotic ingredients, and create fresh applications for familiar ones, to make their meals more interesting. And they enjoy having guests participate in the preparation process whenever possible.

Menu 1 begins with mussels flavored with garlic, shallots, and mint, and sprinkled with a colorful, confetti-like vegetable vinaigrette. After this course, allow guests to select their own toppings for individual pizzas, which are made with pita bread rather than traditional pizza dough to save time. The accompanying salad features romaine, tomatoes, avocado, peppers, and corn tossed with a spicy lime dressing.

Guests also participate in Menu 2 by making their own "wrap-ups" from a variety of ingredients. Various greens and corn tortillas are provided as wrappers for premade fillings of seafood, beef, and chicken, along with a selection of sauces and garnishes. The guests pick and choose their own combinations.

Menu 3 is another ideal late-night meal because its unique mix of flavors and textures wakes up any palate. David Kimmel and Steven Petusevsky marinate half of the chicken wings in an Indian-style curry sauce and the other half in an Italian-style parsley and Parmesan sauce. Orzo, a Greek pasta, and a French country dish of braised scallions with bacon are the accompaniments.

Guests can eat as much or as little as they like at this casual supper featuring steamed mussels in a vegetable vinaigrette, mini-pizzas with a variety of toppings, and a colorful salad.

Mussels with Confetti Vinaigrette
Mediterranean Pita Pizzas
Southwest Salad Bowl

Flat, disk-shaped pita bread, made with either white or whole-wheat flour, is sold in most supermarkets, Middle Eastern bakeries, and health food stores. You can refrigerate it for up to five days or store it in the freezer indefinitely.

WHAT TO DRINK

The cooks prefer a dry, fruity white wine with this menu. A Riesling from California, New York State, or Alsace would be fine.

SHOPPING LIST AND STAPLES

3 pounds mussels
¼ pound sliced boiled ham
¼ pound sweet Italian sausage
¼ pound pepperoni
Large head romaine lettuce
2 medium-size tomatoes (about 1 pound total weight)
Medium-size avocado
Small bunch celery
Small yellow squash
1 small and 1 medium-size green bell pepper
1 small and 1 medium-size red bell pepper
Small carrot
Small yellow onion
Small bunch scallions
1 shallot
3 medium-size cloves garlic
1 bunch parsley
Small bunch each mint, oregano, and basil
2 large lemons
2 limes
¼ pound Montrachet or other goat cheese
¼ pound Gruyère cheese
10-ounce package frozen corn kernels
16-ounce can peeled tomatoes
8-ounce can water chestnuts
7-ounce can tuna
2-ounce tin anchovy fillets
2-ounce jar capers
2¼-ounce jar pitted green olives
3½-ounce can pitted black olives
1 cup plus 3 tablespoons olive oil, approximately
½ cup vegetable or corn oil

2 tablespoons Dijon mustard
4 small plain or whole-wheat pita breads
Pinch of sugar
1½ teaspoons chili powder
1 teaspoon ground coriander
½ teaspoon sweet paprika
½ teaspoon Cayenne pepper, approximately
Salt and freshly ground white pepper
1 cup dry white wine

UTENSILS

Food processor or blender (optional)
Large heavy-gauge nonaluminum saucepan or stockpot with cover
11 x 17-inch cookie sheet
Salad bowl
Large bowl
5 small bowls
Small strainer
Measuring cups and spoons
Chef's knife
Paring knife
2 wooden spoons or salad servers
Slotted spoon
Metal spatula
Stiff scrubbing brush
Grater (if not using processor)

START-TO-FINISH STEPS

One hour ahead: Set out frozen corn to thaw for salad recipe.

1. Peel and mince garlic for mussels and pizza recipes. Peel and mince shallot for mussels recipe. Prepare herbs for mussels, vinaigrette, and pizza recipes. Juice lemons for vinaigrette recipe and limes for salad recipe.
2. Follow mussels recipe step 1 and salad recipe steps 1 through 3.
3. Follow vinaigrette recipe steps 1 through 5.
4. Follow pizza recipe steps 1 through 5.
5. Follow mussels recipe step 2 and pizza recipe steps 6 and 7.
6. Follow mussels recipe steps 3 through 5, and serve as first course.
7. Follow pizza recipe step 8, salad recipe step 4, and serve.

Mussels with Confetti Vinaigrette

3 pounds mussels
1 cup dry white wine
1 shallot, peeled and minced
2 cloves garlic, peeled and minced
1 tablespoon freshly ground white pepper
4 mint sprigs
¼ cup firmly packed parsley sprigs
Confetti Vinaigrette (see following recipe)

1. With stiff brush, scrub mussels under cold running water; remove beards and discard. Scrub again to remove any remaining encrustation. Place mussels in large bowl with enough cold water to cover, and set aside.
2. In heavy-gauge nonaluminum stockpot, bring wine, shallot, garlic, and pepper to a rapid boil over high heat.
3. Discard any mussels with open shells. Add remaining mussels, mint, and parsley to pot, cover, and steam about 5 minutes, or until mussels have opened and flesh is firm.
4. With slotted spoon, transfer mussels to large serving bowl, discarding any with unopened shells.
5. Pour confetti vinaigrette over mussels and serve.

Confetti Vinaigrette

½ small carrot, peeled and trimmed
¼ stalk celery
¼ small red bell pepper
½ small yellow squash
5 water chestnuts
2 tablespoons minced parsley
2 teaspoons minced mint
⅓ cup lemon juice
2 tablespoons Dijon mustard
Pinch of sugar
Salt and freshly ground white pepper to taste
1 cup olive oil

1. Coarsely chop carrot, celery, pepper, and squash.
2. Rinse water chestnuts in strainer; drain and set aside.
3. Combine vegetables in food processor or blender, and dice finely. Or dice vegetables with chef's knife.
4. Combine vegetables with remaining ingredients, except oil, in small bowl and stir to combine.
5. Beating with fork, slowly add oil and continue beating until well blended. Set aside until ready to use.

Mediterranean Pita Pizzas

Small yellow onion
Small green bell pepper
¼ pound sliced boiled ham
¼ pound pepperoni
16-ounce can peeled tomatoes
1 cup pitted green olives
¼ pound sweet Italian sausage
¼ pound Montrachet or other goat cheese
¼ pound Gruyère

7-ounce can tuna
2-ounce tin anchovy fillets
2-ounce jar capers
4 small plain or whole-wheat pita breads
1 tablespoon each minced garlic, oregano, and basil
½ teaspoon Cayenne pepper, approximately
3 tablespoons olive oil, approximately

1. Preheat oven to 450 degrees.
2. Halve and peel onion. Dice one half; reserve remainder for another use. Halve, core, seed, and dice pepper. Stack ham and dice. Cut pepperoni into ⅛-inch-thick slices. Drain tomatoes and chop finely. Drain and dice olives.
3. Remove sausage from casing and crumble. Crumble goat cheese into small bowl.
4. Using food processor or grater, shred Gruyère.
5. Drain tuna and turn into small bowl; flake with fork. Drain anchovies. Rinse capers in small strainer and drain.
6. Split pitas to make 8 rounds. Arrange pitas, cut-side up, on cookie sheet and toast in oven 1 minute, or until edges are slightly brown.
7. Remove pitas from oven and set aside.
8. Divide tomatoes among pitas and sprinkle with garlic, oregano, basil, and Cayenne to taste. Top pitas with cheeses and any combination of onion, green pepper, olives, ham, pepperoni, sausage, tuna, anchovies, and capers. Drizzle pizzas with oil and place in oven 1 minute, or until cheese is bubbly and toppings are heated through; allow 2 to 3 minutes for pizzas with sausage.

Southwest Salad Bowl

Large head romaine lettuce
2 medium-size tomatoes (about 1 pound total weight)
Medium-size green bell pepper
Medium-size red bell pepper
½ medium-size avocado, peeled
4 scallions
½ cup pitted black olives
½ cup frozen corn kernels, thawed
3 tablespoons lime juice
1½ teaspoons chili powder
1 teaspoon ground coriander
½ teaspoon sweet paprika
Salt
½ cup vegetable or corn oil

1. Tear lettuce into bite-size pieces and place in large salad bowl. Dice tomatoes, peppers, and avocado, and add to bowl. Finely chop scallions and add to bowl. Drain olives and add to bowl. Add corn and toss salad to combine. Cover bowl with plastic wrap and refrigerate until ready to serve.
2. Combine lime juice, chili powder, coriander, paprika, and salt to taste in small bowl; stir with fork until blended.
3. Beating with fork, add oil in a slow, steady stream and continue beating until well blended; set aside.
4. Just before serving, stir dressing to recombine. Pour dressing over salad and toss until evenly coated.

Late-night Wrap-ups

Ready for rolling and saucing: chicken in a radicchio wrapper, seafood in Boston lettuce, and beef in a corn tortilla.

Although the list of ingredients for this meal may seem long, the meal itself is easy to prepare and assemble. If you wish, make the fillings a day ahead and refrigerate them until serving time.

In addition to the wrappers suggested, you can use red leaf lettuce, bread with the crusts trimmed, sheets of dried seaweed, or crêpes. For the garnishes, use any or all as suggested, or substitute other colorful vegetables.

WHAT TO DRINK

Light or dark imported or domestic beer is the best partner for this serve-yourself fare.

SHOPPING LIST AND STAPLES

1 pound boneless, skinless chicken breasts, halved
¾ pound beef flank, sirloin, or lean skirt steak
½ pound bay scallops
1 head Boston lettuce
Small bunch spinach
Small head radicchio

Small tomato
Small bunch celery
1 red bell pepper
1 green bell pepper
Small carrot
Small yellow squash
Small yellow onion
Small bunch scallions
1 shallot
3 cloves garlic
1-inch piece fresh ginger
1 bunch parsley
½ pint heavy cream
4 fresh corn tortillas, or 1 package frozen
10-ounce package frozen peas
½-pound package small frozen, peeled shrimp
1 tablespoon tomato paste
½ cup peanut oil, approximately
1 tablespoon Oriental sesame oil
1 teaspoon red wine vinegar
⅓ cup ketchup
1 teaspoon soy sauce

58

1 teaspoon Worcestershire sauce
6-ounce jar chunky-style peanut butter
4-ounce jar roasted unsalted peanuts
16-ounce jar barbecue sauce
8-ounce jar mango chutney
15-ounce bottle hoisin sauce
12-ounce bottle chili sauce
1 teaspoon granulated sugar
½ teaspoon dried oregano
¾ teaspoon ground cumin
¼ teaspoon chili powder
Cayenne pepper
Salt and freshly ground white pepper
2 tablespoons dry sherry
¼ cup plus 1 tablespoon dry white wine

UTENSILS

Food processor (optional)
Large heavy-gauge sauté pan or nonaluminum skillet
Medium-size bowl
3 small bowls
Colander
Measuring cups and spoons
Chef's knife
Paring knife
3 wooden spoons
Slotted spoon
Metal spatula

START-TO-FINISH STEPS

One hour ahead: Thaw shrimp for seafood filling recipe in bowl with cold water. Thaw peas for chicken filling recipe.

Thirty minutes ahead: If using frozen tortillas for wrap-ups recipe, set out to thaw.

1. Peel and mince garlic for beef filling and shallot for seafood filling. Wash and dry parsley. Chop enough parsley to measure 2 tablespoons for seafood filling.
2. Follow beef filling recipe steps 1 through 3.
3. Follow chicken filling recipe steps 1 through 6.
4. Follow wrap-ups recipe steps 1 through 8.
5. Follow beef filling recipe steps 4 and 5, chicken filling recipe steps 7 and 8, and seafood filling recipe steps 1 and 2.
6. One filling at a time, follow beef filling recipe steps 6 through 12, chicken filling recipe steps 9 through 13, and seafood filling recipe steps 3 through 8.
7. Follow wrap-ups recipe steps 9 through 13 and serve.

RECIPES

Late-night Wrap-ups

Wrappers:
1 head Boston lettuce
Small head radicchio
4 fresh corn tortillas, or 4 frozen, thawed

Garnishes:
Small bunch spinach
Small carrot
Small yellow squash

Fillings (see following recipes):
Oriental Chicken
Creamy Seafood
Spicy Beef

Sauces:
8-ounce jar mango chutney
16-ounce jar barbecue sauce
12-ounce bottle chili sauce
15-ounce bottle hoisin sauce

1. Preheat oven to 200 degrees.
2. Wash and dry lettuce. Remove and discard any bruised or discolored leaves. Wrap lettuce in paper towels and refrigerate until ready to serve.
3. Rinse and dry radicchio. Remove and discard any bruised or wilted leaves. Wrap radicchio in paper towels and refrigerate until ready to serve.
4. Stack tortillas, wrap tightly in foil, and place in oven to warm.
5. Prepare garnishes: Wash spinach thoroughly in several changes of cold water and dry. Remove and discard tough stems. Stack leaves and shred enough spinach crosswise to measure 1 cup.
6. Peel and trim carrot. Halve crosswise; set aside.
7. Wash and dry squash. Trim ends and discard. Halve lengthwise, then cut each half crosswise into thirds.
8. Using food processor, shred carrot and squash. Or, using chef's knife, cut carrot and squash into ¼-inch julienne.
9. Arrange spinach, carrot, and squash for garnishes on serving platter.
10. Arrange radicchio and lettuce leaves on second platter.
11. Turn dipping sauces into individual small bowls.
12. Remove tortillas from oven and transfer to platter with lettuce and radicchio.
13. To serve, let guests select any combination of wrappers, fillings, garnishes, and sauces, and roll them up, if desired. The sauces may also be used for dipping the wrap-ups.

Oriental Chicken Filling

1 tablespoon Oriental sesame oil
1 teaspoon soy sauce
2 tablespoons dry sherry
2 cloves garlic
1-inch piece fresh ginger
1 pound boneless, skinless chicken breasts, halved
2 stalks celery
Small bunch scallions
1 tablespoon plus 1 teaspoon peanut oil
½ cup roasted unsalted peanuts
2 teaspoons chunky-style peanut butter

¼ cup dry white wine
¼ cup frozen peas, thawed
Salt
Cayenne pepper

1. For marinade, combine sesame oil, soy sauce, and 1 tablespoon sherry in small bowl and stir with fork to blend; set aside.
2. Bruise garlic under flat blade of chef's knife. Remove peel and discard; set garlic aside.
3. Cut ¼-inch-thick slice from ginger and peel; reserve remaining ginger for another use.
4. Rinse chicken and dry with paper towels. Using chef's knife, cut chicken into 1-inch chunks.
5. Combine garlic, ginger, and chicken in container of food processor fitted with steel blade and process, pulsing machine on and off two or three times, until chicken is minced; do *not* overprocess. Or, mince garlic, ginger, and chicken with chef's knife.
6. Add chicken mixture to marinade and set aside, stirring occasionally, 10 to 15 minutes.
7. Wash and dry celery. Dice enough to measure 1 cup.
8. Wash and dry scallions. Finely chop enough to measure 1 cup.
9. In large heavy-gauge sauté pan or nonaluminum skillet, heat 1 tablespoon peanut oil over medium-high heat 45 seconds, or until almost smoking. With slotted spoon, transfer chicken mixture to pan and sauté, stirring, 4 to 5 minutes, or until chicken is opaque and nearly cooked.
10. Return chicken mixture to small bowl; set aside.
11. Add remaining teaspoon peanut oil to pan and heat over medium-high heat. Add celery, scallions, and peanuts, and sauté, stirring frequently, 1 to 2 minutes, or until celery begins to soften.
12. Add peanut butter, white wine, and remaining tablespoon sherry to pan, and stir to blend. If too thick, stir in water, 1 tablespoon at a time, to achieve desired consistency.
13. Add chicken mixture, with any accumulated juices, and peas to peanut butter mixture, and stir to combine. Season with salt and Cayenne pepper to taste. Return mixture to small bowl and set aside until ready to serve.

Creamy Seafood Filling

½-pound package small frozen, peeled shrimp, thawed
½ pound bay scallops
Small tomato
1 tablespoon peanut oil
1 shallot, peeled and minced
1 tablespoon tomato paste
1 tablespoon dry white wine
¼ cup heavy cream
1 teaspoon Worcestershire sauce
2 tablespoons chopped parsley
Salt and freshly ground white pepper

1. Place shrimp and scallops in colander and rinse, drain, and pat dry with paper towels.
2. Wash and dry tomato. Core, halve, seed, and dice.

3. In large heavy-gauge sauté pan or nonaluminum skillet, heat oil over medium-high heat 45 seconds, or until almost smoking.
4. Add shrimp and scallops, and sauté, stirring, about 2 minutes, or until almost opaque.
5. Add minced shallot and tomato paste, and sauté, stirring, another 2 minutes.
6. Add diced tomato, white wine, and cream, and cook over medium-high heat, stirring occasionally, 2 to 3 minutes, or until mixture is thick enough to coat back of wooden spoon.
7. Add Worcestershire sauce, parsley, and salt and pepper to taste, and stir to combine.
8. Turn mixture into small bowl and set aside until ready to serve.

Spicy Beef Filling

¾ pound beef flank, sirloin, or lean skirt steak
1 teaspoon minced garlic
¾ teaspoon ground cumin
½ teaspoon dried oregano
¼ teaspoon chili powder
¼ cup peanut oil
1 red bell pepper
1 green bell pepper
Small yellow onion
⅓ cup ketchup
1 teaspoon red wine vinegar
1 teaspoon granulated sugar

1. Cut beef into long ½-inch-wide strips; set aside.
2. Combine ½ teaspoon garlic, cumin, oregano, chili powder, and 1 tablespoon peanut oil in small bowl, and stir with fork to blend.
3. Add beef strips and toss with spice mixture until evenly coated. Set aside to marinate at least 15 minutes.
4. Wash and dry bell peppers. Core and seed peppers. Cut crosswise into ¼-inch-wide rings.
5. Halve and peel onion. Cut crosswise into ¼-inch-thick slices.
6. In large heavy-gauge sauté pan or nonaluminum skillet, heat 2 tablespoons peanut oil over medium-high heat 45 seconds, or until almost smoking.
7. Add marinated beef to pan and do not disturb for 1 minute, or until juices start to appear on surface. With metal spatula, turn beef and brown another minute.
8. Transfer beef and cooking juices to small bowl.
9. Add remaining tablespoon peanut oil to pan and heat over medium-high heat 45 seconds, or until almost smoking.
10. Add peppers, onion, and remaining ½ teaspoon garlic, and sauté, stirring occasionally, 3 minutes, or until vegetables are slightly softened.
11. Add ketchup, red wine vinegar, and sugar, and stir to combine.
12. Return sautéed beef with any accumulated juices to pan, and stir to combine. Transfer mixture to small bowl and set aside until ready to serve.

Marinated Chicken Wings in Two Flavors
Lemon Orzo
Bacon-Braised Scallions

This casual meal is packed with zesty flavors: The baked chicken wings are prepared with curry and parsley-Parmesan marinades; the orzo is flavored with lemon; and the scallions are braised with bacon and herbs.

Chicken wings have become so popular recently that they are being packaged separately by many supermarkets. Fresh wings, like chicken in general, should be moist and odor free. For maximum flavor, marinate the wings for several hours or overnight. If they are not totally immersed in the marinade, turn them from time to time so that both sides absorb the flavors.

Orzo, a small pasta popular in Greece, resembles rice in its uncooked state, though the grains are double the size of rice when cooked.

WHAT TO DRINK

A lightly chilled, light-bodied rosé is your best bet with these dishes. A good choice would be a rosé d'Anjou.

SHOPPING LIST AND STAPLES

16 chicken wings (about 3½ pounds total weight)
4 slices bacon (about ¼ pound)
1 carrot
2 bunches scallions
1-inch piece fresh ginger
2 cloves garlic
1 bunch parsley
2 large lemons
2 ounces Parmesan cheese
1½ cups chicken stock, preferably homemade
   (see page 8), or canned
½ cup peanut oil
⅓ cup plus 1 teaspoon olive oil
1 teaspoon Dijon mustard
3½-ounce can pitted black olives
8-ounce package orzo
1 tablespoon curry powder
1 teaspoon ground cumin
½ teaspoon ground turmeric
½ teaspoon dried thyme
1 bay leaf
Salt
Freshly ground white and black pepper

UTENSILS

Food processor or blender
Large heavy-gauge sauté pan with cover
2 medium-size saucepans

61

Small saucepan
13 x 9-inch baking pan
Large nonaluminum bowl
2 medium-size nonaluminum bowls
Small bowl
Large strainer
Measuring cups and spoons
Chef's knife
Paring knife
Wooden spoon
Metal tongs
Grater
Zester (if not using grater)
Basting brush

START-TO-FINISH STEPS

1. Wash and dry 1 lemon. With zester or grater, remove enough rind, avoiding white pith, to measure 1 teaspoon for orzo recipe. Halve both lemons crosswise and squeeze enough juice to measure ¼ cup for orzo recipe and 1 tablespoon for chicken recipe. Wash and dry scallions. Set aside 2 scallions for chicken recipe and remainder for braised scallions recipe. Wash and dry parsley. Measure ½ cup loosely packed sprigs for chicken recipe and mince enough parsley to measure 1 tablespoon for orzo recipe.
2. Follow chicken recipe steps 1 through 11.
3. Follow orzo recipe step 1 and braised scallions recipe steps 1 through 3.
4. While stock is simmering, follow orzo recipe step 2 and chicken recipe step 12.
5. While orzo is cooking and chicken is baking, follow braised scallions recipe steps 4 through 6.
6. While scallions are cooking, follow orzo recipe step 3 and chicken recipe step 13.
7. Follow orzo recipe steps 4 through 6.
8. Follow braised scallions recipe step 7 and chicken recipe step 14, and serve with orzo.

RECIPES

Marinated Chicken Wings in Two Flavors

16 chicken wings (about 3½ pounds total weight)

Curry Marinade:
1-inch piece fresh ginger
¼ cup peanut oil

1 tablespoon lemon juice
1 tablespoon curry powder
1 teaspoon ground cumin
1 teaspoon Dijon mustard
Salt

Parsley-Parmesan Marinade:
2 cloves garlic
2 scallions, washed and trimmed
2 ounces Parmesan cheese
½ cup loosely packed parsley sprigs
Salt
Freshly ground white pepper
⅓ cup olive oil

1. Rinse chicken wings under cold running water and dry with paper towels; set aside.
2. For curry marinade, peel and mince enough ginger to measure 1 teaspoon.
3. Combine ginger, peanut oil, lemon juice, curry powder, cumin, mustard, and salt to taste in medium-size nonaluminum bowl, and stir with fork to blend; set aside.
4. For parsley-Parmesan marinade, bruise garlic under flat blade of chef's knife; remove peel and discard. Halve garlic and set aside.
5. Cut scallions into 1-inch-long pieces.
6. Using food processor fitted with steel blade, or grater, grate enough cheese to measure ½ cup. Turn cheese into small bowl and set aside.
7. In food processor or blender, combine garlic, scallions, and parsley, and process, turning machine on and off several times, until ingredients are minced.
8. Add Parmesan cheese, salt and pepper to taste, and process just until combined.
9. With machine running, slowly add olive oil and process until oil is totally incorporated and marinade is smooth. Transfer marinade to medium-size nonaluminum bowl and set aside.
10. Add 8 chicken wings to each marinade and turn until evenly coated. Set aside to marinate at least 10 minutes.
11. Meanwhile, preheat oven to 475 degrees.
12. Arrange wings in single layer in baking pan and bake, uncovered, basting occasionally with respective marinades, about 10 minutes on one side, or until browned.
13. Using tongs, turn wings and bake another 10 minutes, or until browned.
14. Divide wings among 4 dinner plates and serve.

Lemon Orzo

Salt
1½ cups orzo
½ cup pitted black olives
¼ cup lemon juice, approximately
1 teaspoon lemon zest
1 teaspoon olive oil
¼ cup peanut oil
1 tablespoon minced parsley
½ teaspoon ground turmeric
Freshly ground white pepper

1. In medium-size saucepan, bring 2 quarts lightly salted water to a boil over high heat.
2. Add orzo to boiling water and cook 10 to 12 minutes, or until *al dente*.
3. Turn orzo into strainer and rinse under cold running water; set aside to drain.
4. Drain and mince olives; set aside.
5. Combine lemon juice, zest, oils, olives, parsley, turmeric, 1½ teaspoons salt, and pepper to taste in large nonaluminum bowl, and stir with fork to blend.
6. Add orzo to dressing and stir to combine. Taste and adjust seasoning, adding more lemon juice or salt and pepper if desired. Set orzo aside until ready to serve.

Bacon-Braised Scallions

1 carrot
4 slices bacon (about ¼ pound)
1½ cups chicken stock
½ teaspoon dried thyme
1 bay leaf
Freshly ground black pepper
2 bunches scallions, approximately, washed and trimmed

1. Peel and trim carrot. Dice enough carrot to measure ¼ cup; set aside.
2. Dice enough bacon to measure ¼ cup; set aside.
3. In small saucepan, bring stock to a gentle simmer over medium heat.
4. Place large heavy-gauge sauté pan over medium-high heat. Add diced bacon and sauté, stirring frequently, 2 to 3 minutes, or until bacon becomes translucent.
5. Add diced carrot, thyme, bay leaf, and pepper to taste to pan with bacon, and sauté, stirring frequently, 3 to 4 minutes, or until bacon begins to brown.
6. Pour off fat from pan. Top bacon mixture with scallions and add just enough hot chicken stock to cover. Bring to a boil over medium-high heat, cover pan, and braise 7 to 8 minutes, or until scallions are tender.
7. Remove and discard bay leaf. Using tongs, divide scallions among dinner plates and top with equal portions of bacon mixture. Serve broth separately, if desired.

ADDED TOUCH

The success of this dessert depends on using a sweet, ripe pineapple: Buy a heavy one that has a deep-golden rind.

Honey-Rum Pineapple with Pistachio Cream

Medium-size pineapple (about 3½ pounds)
½ cup shelled pistachio nuts
1 orange
¼ cup honey
1½ cups 80-proof golden rum
½ teaspoon vanilla extract
½ pint heavy cream
2 tablespoons confectioners' sugar

1. Place medium-size bowl and beaters in freezer.
2. Preheat oven to 450 degrees.
3. With chef's knife, trim ends from pineapple. Stand pineapple upright and, holding it firmly, trim off rind in vertical strips, turning pineapple as you go. Halve pineapple lengthwise; cut out core and discard. Cut halves crosswise into ½-inch slices and set aside in flameproof dish.
4. Arrange pistachio nuts in a single layer on baking sheet and toast in oven, shaking pan occasionally to prevent scorching, about 4 minutes, or until lightly browned.
5. Wash and dry orange. Using zester or grater, remove rind, avoiding white pith as much as possible. Halve orange crosswise and juice; set aside.
6. In medium-size nonaluminum bowl, combine honey, rum, vanilla, and orange juice and zest, and stir to blend. Pour mixture over pineapple and set aside to macerate 15 minutes.
7. Remove pistachio nuts from oven and transfer to clean kitchen towel. Turn on broiler. Rub pistachios gently to remove skins; chop coarsely and set aside.
8. Broil macerated pineapple 2 to 3 inches from heating element for 8 to 10 minutes, or until lightly browned.
9. In chilled bowl, whip cream until soft peaks form. Sprinkle in sugar and whip cream until stiff.
10. Gently fold in half of the chopped pistachios.
11. Divide pineapple among 4 dessert plates, top each with whipped cream and pistachios, and serve.

Alice Gautsch and Jane Morimoto

As full-time working women, Jane Morimoto and Alice Gautsch know that having a career and cooking appetizing meals every day can be difficult. Therefore, they have adopted a practical cooking philosophy: Achieve the maximum from food in minimum time. They see recipes as road maps designed to guide a cook—*directly*—to fine food preparation and presentation. The menus they present here are designed to fit into today's fast-paced lifestyle. They are simple and straightforward, featuring a wide range of ingredients in dishes that are delicious yet not time-consuming to prepare.

Menu 2 is an impressive buffet that will please supper guests at any time of year. Clams in their shells, crabmeat, and fish flavor the quick-cooking and savory soup, which is best served from a large tureen. The soup is supplemented by a colorful California-style salad that includes avocado and a variety of bell peppers.

Menus 1 and 3 celebrate seasonal produce. The mélange of vegetables in Menu 1 is made up of eggplant, tomatoes, and peppers—all abundantly available in the summer months. With it, the cooks serve steak flavored with rosemary and black pepper, and a first course of fettuccine tossed with pistachios.

Menu 3 is a tribute to spring, with a light main course of fresh artichokes and homemade mustard mayonnaise, accompanied by a chicken-vegetable soup that includes fresh asparagus. The dessert is strawberries in a lemon syrup.

Slices of steak, a mélange of vegetables with black olives, and pasta with herbs and pistachios make an elegant but easy supper for family or friends. A dry red wine is the appropriate beverage with this meal.

Fettuccine with Pistachio Sauce
Rosemary-Pepper Steak
Mélange of Summer Vegetables

New York strip steaks, or beef loin top loin steaks, are very tender and are best when cooked quickly. Grapeseed oil is ideal for pan frying the steaks because of its high smoking point. Purchase this oil at specialty food stores, or use olive or vegetable oil instead.

WHAT TO DRINK

A slightly soft and dry red wine would make the best foil for these dishes. The cooks suggest a French Beaujolais or a young Merlot from Washington or Oregon.

SHOPPING LIST AND STAPLES

Two ¾-inch-thick boneless New York strip steaks
    (about 12 ounces each)
Small eggplant (about 6 ounces)
2 large plum tomatoes or small regular tomatoes
Small green bell pepper, or 2 fresh mild Anaheim
    chilies
Small onion
Large shallot
1 clove garlic
Small bunch fresh parsley
Small bunch fresh oregano, or ½ teaspoon
    dried
4 tablespoons unsalted butter
6 ounces Parmesan cheese
½ cup olive oil, approximately
4-ounce bottle grapeseed oil
2 tablespoons red wine vinegar
4-ounce can pitted black olives
½ pound fresh fettuccine, or 4 ounces dried
6-ounce package shelled natural pistachios
1 teaspoon dried rosemary
Salt and freshly ground black pepper
1 tablespoon whole black peppercorns

UTENSILS

Food processor (optional)
Stockpot
Large sauté pan
2 medium-size heavy-gauge skillets
Small broiler pan
Large nonaluminum bowl
2 small bowls, 1 nonaluminum

Colander
Measuring cups and spoons
Chef's knife
Carving knife
Paring knife
2 wooden spoons
Metal spatula
Metal tongs
Pastry brush
Mortar and pestle (optional)
Rolling pin (if not using mortar and pestle)
Grater (if not using food processor)

START-TO-FINISH STEPS

1. Follow steak recipe steps 1 through 4.
2. Follow pasta recipe steps 1 through 11 and serve as first course.
3. Follow steak recipe step 5.
4. While steak is cooking, follow vegetables recipe steps 1 through 4.
5. Follow steak recipe step 6.
6. Follow vegetables recipe steps 5 through 7.
7. Follow steak recipe step 7.
8. While steak is resting, follow vegetables recipe steps 8 through 11.
9. Follow steak recipe step 8, and serve with vegetables.

RECIPES

Fettuccine with Pistachio Sauce

1 tablespoon salt
Small bunch fresh parsley
Small bunch fresh oregano, or ½ teaspoon dried
6 ounces Parmesan cheese
½ pound fresh fettuccine, or 4 ounces dried
6-ounce package shelled natural pistachios
Large shallot
1 clove garlic
4 tablespoons unsalted butter
2 tablespoons olive oil
Freshly ground black pepper

1. Bring 3 quarts water and salt to a boil in stockpot over high heat.
2. Meanwhile, wash parsley, and fresh oregano if using,

and dry with paper towels. Trim stems and discard. Mince enough parsley to measure ¼ cup and enough oregano to measure 1 tablespoon; set aside. Reserve remaining herbs for another use.

3. In food processor fitted with steel blade, or with grater, grate enough Parmesan to measure ¾ cup; set aside.

4. Add fettuccine to boiling water and stir to separate strands. Cook 2 to 3 minutes for fresh, 5 to 7 minutes for dried, or just until *al dente*.

5. Meanwhile, chop enough pistachios to measure ¼ cup; set aside.

6. Peel shallot and cut enough into slivers to measure 2 tablespoons. Peel and mince garlic.

7. Turn fettuccine into colander and set aside to drain.

8. In large sauté pan, heat butter and oil over medium-high heat. Add shallot and garlic, and sauté, stirring, 2 minutes.

9. Stir in fresh or dried oregano, and pepper to taste.

10. Reduce heat to medium, add drained fettuccine, and sauté, tossing to combine, 2 minutes, or until heated through.

11. Add parsley, Parmesan cheese, and pistachios, and toss to combine. Divide fettuccine among 4 bowls and serve.

Rosemary-Pepper Steak

1 tablespoon whole black peppercorns
1 teaspoon dried rosemary
Two ¾-inch-thick boneless New York strip steaks
  (about 12 ounces each)
Salt
2 tablespoons grapeseed oil

1. Crack peppercorns under flat blade of chef's knife; set aside.

2. Crush rosemary with mortar and pestle, or place between 2 sheets of waxed paper and crush with rolling pin.

3. In small bowl, combine cracked pepper and rosemary.

4. Season steaks on both sides with salt; smear both sides of each steak with pepper mixture, pressing with fingers to help mixture adhere; set aside.

5. Heat 1 tablespoon oil in each of 2 medium-size heavy-gauge skillets over medium-high heat until very hot. Add steaks and cook 4 minutes on 1 side for rare, 5 minutes for medium rare, or 7 minutes for well done.

6. Using tongs, turn steaks and cook another 4 to 7 minutes for desired degree of doneness.

7. Transfer steaks to cutting board, cover loosely with foil, and allow to rest at least 5 minutes.

8. Cut steaks into ½-inch-thick slices and divide among 4 dinner plates.

Mélange of Summer Vegetables

Small eggplant (about 6 ounces)
⅓ cup plus 2 tablespoons olive oil
2 tablespoons red wine vinegar
Salt and freshly ground black pepper
2 large plum tomatoes or small regular tomatoes
Small green bell pepper, or 2 fresh mild Anaheim chilies
Small onion
½ cup pitted black olives

1. Preheat broiler.

2. Wash and dry eggplant. Trim ends and discard. Cut eggplant crosswise into ¼-inch-thick slices and arrange in single layer in broiler pan. Brush eggplant with 1 tablespoon olive oil and broil 4 inches from heating element 5 minutes.

3. While eggplant is broiling, combine ⅓ cup oil, vinegar, ½ teaspoon salt, and pepper to taste in small nonaluminum bowl and beat with fork to blend; set aside.

4. Wash and dry tomatoes. If using regular tomatoes, core. Cut into wedges and place in large nonaluminum bowl.

5. Using metal spatula, turn eggplant slices, brush with remaining tablespoon olive oil, and broil another 5 minutes, or until tender.

6. Meanwhile, wearing rubber gloves if using chilies, rinse chilies or green bell pepper under cold running water and dry with paper towels. Core and seed bell pepper or chilies. Cut crosswise into ¼-inch-thick rings; add to bowl with tomatoes.

7. Remove eggplant from broiler and set aside to cool.

8. Halve and peel onion. Cut crosswise into ¼-inch-thick slices; add to bowl with vegetables.

9. Drain olives and add to bowl.

10. Add eggplant to bowl.

11. Stir dressing to recombine and pour over vegetables. Stir gently until vegetables are evenly coated.

ADDED TOUCH

This delicious dessert coffee can be made with regular or decaffeinated coffee, depending on the desires of your guests.

Orange-Almond Dessert Coffee

¼ cup sliced almonds
3 cups freshly brewed coffee
½ teaspoon grated orange rind
½ pint vanilla ice cream
¼ cup orange liqueur
¼ cup almond liqueur

1. Preheat oven to 350 degrees.

2. Arrange almonds in single layer on baking sheet and toast in oven, shaking pan occasionally to prevent scorching, 8 to 10 minutes, or until lightly browned.

3. Meanwhile, using your favorite method, brew coffee.

4. Remove almonds from oven and set aside to cool.

5. Place pinch of grated rind in each of four 8-ounce glasses or coffee mugs.

6. Add scoop of ice cream, 1 tablespoon each orange and almond liqueurs, and ¾ cup coffee to each glass or mug.

7. Top each drink with 1 tablespoon toasted almonds and serve.

California Salad
Savory Fish Soup
Saffron-Herb Bread

Champagne and fresh flowers give a celebratory feeling to this buffet of seafood soup, tossed salad, and saffron-herb bread.

More like a stew than a soup, the substantial seafood main course contains chunks of white fish and shell-fish, as well as clams in their shells. However, you can use whatever seafood you like, keeping the proportions the same. Fresh snow peas, or Chinese pea pods, sold at Oriental groceries and many supermarkets, add color and texture to the soup. They will keep for a day or two in a plastic bag in the refrigerator.

WHAT TO DRINK

A crisp, dry, sparkling wine, either imported or domestic, would add elegance to this flavorful menu. If you prefer a still wine, try a well-chilled Gewürztraminer.

SHOPPING LIST AND STAPLES

12 small fresh clams
½ pound fillet of sea bass, cod, or other white-fleshed fish
¼ pound fresh or frozen lump crabmeat
Small jícama root (optional)
¼ pound snow peas
Medium-size avocado
1 each small green, red, and yellow bell pepper

1 head Bibb lettuce
Large tomato
Small cucumber
Small yellow onion
2 medium-size leeks
1 clove garlic
Small bunch fresh parsley
Small bunch fresh coriander (optional)
Small bunch fresh chives, or 2-ounce container frozen
1 lemon
1 navel orange
1 stick unsalted butter
Three 8-ounce bottles clam juice
6 tablespoons olive oil
3 tablespoons vegetable oil
3 tablespoons white wine vinegar
Hot pepper sauce
1 small loaf French bread
¼ teaspoon sugar
½ teaspoon dried thyme
½ teaspoon dried oregano
Pinch of powdered saffron
Salt and freshly ground pepper
1 cup dry white wine

UTENSILS

Heavy-gauge nonaluminum stockpot
Broiler pan with rack
2 medium-size bowls, 1 nonaluminum
2 small bowls
Medium-size serving platter
Strainer
Measuring cups and spoons
Chef's knife
Serrated bread knife
Paring knife
Wooden spoon
Kitchen shears
Stiff scrubbing brush
Grater or zester

START-TO-FINISH STEPS

One hour ahead: If using frozen crabmeat for soup recipe, immerse in cold water to thaw.

Thirty minutes ahead: Set out butter to come to room temperature for bread recipe.

1. Wash parsley, and other fresh herbs if using, and dry with paper towels. Trim stems from parsley and coriander, and discard. Mince enough parsley to measure 1 tablespoon for bread recipe. Coarsely chop enough coriander or parsley to measure 1 tablespoon for soup recipe. Snip enough chives to measure 1 tablespoon for salad recipe. Reserve remaining herbs for another use. Wash lemon and dry with paper towel. Grate enough rind to measure 2 teaspoons for soup recipe and squeeze juice of whole

lemon for salad recipe; set aside.
2. Follow bread recipe step 1 and salad recipe steps 1 through 8.
3. Follow soup recipe steps 1 through 5 and bread recipe step 2.
4. Follow soup recipe steps 6 through 14 and bread recipe steps 3 through 5.
5. Follow salad recipe step 9, soup recipe step 15, and serve with bread.

RECIPES

California Salad

3 tablespoons olive oil
3 tablespoons vegetable oil
3 tablespoons white wine vinegar
1 tablespoon snipped fresh or frozen
    chives
½ teaspoon salt
¼ teaspoon sugar
Freshly ground pepper
1 each small green, red, and yellow
    bell pepper
1 head Bibb lettuce
Small jícama root (optional)
1 navel orange
Medium-size avocado
Juice of 1 lemon

1. For dressing, combine oils, vinegar, chives, salt, sugar, and pepper to taste in small bowl and beat with fork until blended; set aside.
2. Wash peppers and dry with paper towels. Core peppers and cut crosswise into ¼-inch-thick rings. Remove and discard seeds and ribs. Place pepper rings in medium-size nonaluminum bowl.
3. Stir dressing to recombine and pour over pepper rings. Toss until evenly coated and set aside for at least 30 minutes.
4. Wash and dry lettuce. Remove and discard any bruised or discolored leaves. Line serving platter with lettuce; set aside.
5. If using jícama, peel and trim ends. Halve lengthwise, then cut each half crosswise into ¼-inch-thick slices. Stack slices and cut into ¼-inch julienne; set aside.
6. Using sharp paring knife, peel orange, removing as much white pith as possible; discard peel. Cut orange crosswise into ¼-inch-thick slices; set aside.
7. Halve avocado lengthwise, cutting around pit. Twist halves in opposite directions to separate. Remove and discard pit. Peel avocado and cut lengthwise into ½-inch-thick slices. Place slices on plate and sprinkle with lemon juice to prevent discoloration; set aside.
8. Arrange jícama, orange, and avocado slices on lettuce-lined platter. Cover with plastic wrap and refrigerate until ready to serve.
9. When ready to serve, spoon peppers and dressing over salad.

Savory Fish Soup

Small yellow onion
1 clove garlic
1 tablespoon olive oil
2 teaspoons grated lemon rind
½ teaspoon dried thyme
Salt
3 cups clam juice
1 cup dry white wine
2 medium-size leeks
Large tomato
Small cucumber
¼ pound snow peas
12 small fresh clams
½ pound fillet of sea bass, cod, or other white-fleshed fish
¼ pound fresh lump crabmeat, or ¼ pound frozen, thawed
Dash of hot pepper sauce
Freshly ground pepper
1 tablespoon coarsely chopped coriander or parsley

1. Halve and peel onion. Chop enough to measure ½ cup.
2. Crush garlic under flat blade of chef's knife. Remove peel and discard.
3. In heavy-gauge nonaluminum stockpot, heat oil over medium-high heat. Add onion and garlic, and sauté, stirring occasionally, 3 minutes, or until tender and golden.
4. Stir in lemon rind, thyme, ½ teaspoon salt, clam juice, wine, and 3 cups water. Bring mixture to a boil and simmer, uncovered, 15 minutes.
5. Prepare leeks: Trim leeks, split lengthwise, and rinse under cold running water. Cut into 1½-inch-long slices, then cut each slice into ¼-inch julienne.
6. Wash and dry tomato. Dice enough to measure 1 cup.
7. Peel cucumber and halve lengthwise. Scoop out seeds and discard. Dice enough cucumber to measure 1 cup.
8. String snow peas; wash, dry, and halve diagonally.
9. Using stiff-bristled brush, scrub clams under cold running water. Discard any opened clams.
10. Pour broth through strainer set over medium-size bowl; discard solids left in strainer.
11. Return 6 cups strained broth to stockpot and bring to a boil. Add clams and simmer, uncovered, 5 minutes.
12. Rinse and dry fish and cut into 1-inch chunks.
13. Place crabmeat in strainer and rinse; drain. Remove and discard any cartilage or bits of shell.
14. Add seafood, vegetables, and hot pepper sauce to pot and simmer another 5 minutes, or until fish flakes easily.
15. Remove and discard any unopened clams. Taste and adjust seasoning. Turn soup into large tureen or bowl and sprinkle with chopped coriander or parsley.

Saffron-Herb Bread

1 stick unsalted butter, at room temperature
2 tablespoons olive oil
1 tablespoon minced parsley
½ teaspoon dried oregano
Pinch of powdered saffron
1 small loaf French bread

1. Combine all ingredients except bread in small bowl and blend with fork. Set aside at least 10 minutes.
2. Preheat broiler.
3. Cut bread into ½- to ¾-inch-thick slices and spread slices with butter mixture.
4. Place bread on broiler rack and broil 4 to 5 inches from heating element 2 to 3 minutes, or until golden brown.
5. Transfer bread to napkin-lined basket.

ADDED TOUCH

A summertime treat, this dessert should be made at the height of the fresh peach season.

Fresh Peach Tart

3 cups peeled, pitted, and sliced fresh peaches
6 tablespoons cream sherry
1 cup peeled, pitted, and chopped fresh peaches
2 tablespoons granulated sugar
Pinch of salt
Pinch of freshly ground nutmeg
2 tablespoons cornstarch
Walnut Tart Shell (see following recipe)
½ pint heavy cream, or 1 pint ice cream (optional)

1. If using heavy cream, place bowl and beaters in freezer.
2. Place sliced peaches in medium-size bowl. Add 2 tablespoons sherry and toss until evenly coated; set aside.
3. To make glaze, combine chopped peaches, ¼ cup sherry, ¼ cup water, sugar, salt, and nutmeg in medium-size saucepan and bring to a boil over medium-high heat. Reduce heat and simmer, uncovered, 15 minutes.
4. Turn mixture into strainer set over medium-size bowl; set syrup aside to cool. Discard solids left in strainer.
5. Add cornstarch to liquid in bowl and stir until dissolved. Return liquid to pan and bring to a boil, stirring, over medium heat. Boil 1 minute, or until mixture thickens.
6. Brush tart shell with small amount of syrupy glaze.
7. Add sliced peaches to remaining glaze and stir to coat.
8. Arrange peaches in tart shell; set aside.
9. If using heavy cream, beat in chilled bowl until stiff.
10. Cut tart into wedges and place on dessert plates. Serve topped with whipped cream or ice cream, if desired.

Walnut Tart Shell

1 cup all-purpose flour
3 tablespoons finely chopped walnuts
2 tablespoons granulated sugar
5 tablespoons unsalted butter, at room temperature
1 egg yolk

1. Preheat oven to 400 degrees.
2. Combine flour, walnuts, and sugar, and stir to blend.
3. Cut in butter until mixture resembles small peas.
4. Add egg yolk and blend with fingers until dough gathers into a loose ball.
5. Place dough in center of 9-inch tart pan with removable bottom. Press dough firmly and evenly over bottom and up sides of pan. Bake crust about 12 minutes, or until golden.

Artichokes with Mustard Mayonnaise
Chicken-Vegetable Soup
Strawberries with Lemon and Mint

A quick yet nourishing late-night meal: artichokes with homemade mayonnaise, chicken-vegetable soup, and fresh strawberries.

Although artichokes are now available on a year-round basis, they are most plentiful and least expensive in the spring. The artichoke is an immature flower head surrounded by fleshy leaves. Select artichokes with firm, solid heads.

WHAT TO DRINK

Artichokes are a difficult companion for many wines. A soft fruity white, such as a dry Chenin Blanc from California or the Pacific Northwest, goes admirably with the soup but might not stand up to the artichokes. A more acidic Italian Pinot Grigio or Verdicchio suits both.

SHOPPING LIST AND STAPLES

1-pound whole chicken breast, with skin and bones
4 medium-size artichokes
6 ounces bok choy or ½ pound fresh spinach
6 ounces asparagus spears
¼ pound mushrooms
Small bunch celery
2 large carrots
Medium-size leek
Medium-size yellow onion
Large clove garlic
Small bunch fresh chives, or 2-ounce container frozen

Small bunch fresh mint, or ¼ teaspoon dried
Small bunch fresh tarragon, or ¼ teaspoon dried
2 lemons
1 pint strawberries
3 cups homemade chicken stock (see page 8), or two
    13¾-ounce cans
1 egg
¾ cup olive oil
1 tablespoon vegetable oil
½ teaspoon Dijon mustard
¼ cup granulated sugar
Salt and freshly ground pepper
½ cup dry white wine

UTENSILS

Food processor or blender
Large deep skillet with steamer unit (optional) and cover
Wire rack to fit inside deep skillet (if not using steamer
    unit)
Large heavy-gauge saucepan with cover
Small heavy-gauge nonaluminum saucepan
Platter
Large bowl
Medium-size bowl
Small bowl
Large strainer
Measuring cups and spoons
Chef's knife
Paring knife
Wooden spoon
Ladle
Rubber spatula
Metal tongs
Kitchen shears
Vegetable peeler

START-TO-FINISH STEPS

1. Rinse and dry fresh herbs, if using. Snip enough chives to measure 1 teaspoon for artichokes recipe. Mince enough tarragon to measure 1 teaspoon for artichokes recipe, and chop enough mint to measure 1 tablespoon for strawberries recipe. Reserve remaining herbs for another use. Wash and dry lemons. Using sharp paring knife, remove peel from lemons, avoiding white pith as much as possible. Julienne enough peel to measure ¼ cup for strawberries recipe; set aside. Halve 1 lemon and squeeze enough juice to measure 1 tablespoon for artichokes recipe and 1 tablespoon for strawberries recipe; set aside.
2. Follow strawberries recipe steps 1 through 3.
3. Follow artichokes recipe steps 1 through 3.
4. Follow soup recipe steps 1 through 8.
5. While soup is simmering, follow artichokes recipe steps 4 through 6.
6. Follow soup recipe steps 9 through 16.
7. Follow artichokes recipe steps 7 and 8.
8. Follow soup recipe step 17 and artichokes recipe step 9.

9. Follow soup recipe step 18 and artichokes recipe step 10, and serve.
10. Follow strawberries recipe step 4 and serve as dessert.

RECIPES

Artichokes with Mustard Mayonnaise

1 egg
½ teaspoon Dijon mustard
¼ teaspoon salt
1 tablespoon lemon juice
1 teaspoon snipped fresh or frozen chives
1 teaspoon minced fresh tarragon, or ¼ teaspoon dried
¾ cup olive oil
4 medium-size artichokes

1. To make mayonnaise, combine egg, mustard, salt, lemon juice, and herbs in food processor or blender and process just until blended.
2. With machine running, add ¼ cup oil, one drop at a time, and continue to process until mixture begins to thicken. Then add remaining oil in a slow, steady stream and process until oil is totally incorporated and mayonnaise is thick and smooth.
3. Using rubber spatula, scrape mayonnaise into small bowl. Taste and add more salt if desired. Cover with plastic wrap and refrigerate until ready to serve.
4. Fill large deep skillet fitted with wire rack or steamer unit with enough cold water to come within ½ inch of rack or steamer unit and bring to a boil over medium-high heat.
5. Meanwhile, pull off lower leaves of artichokes; trim stems. Cut off top quarter of each artichoke and discard. Snip tips of remaining leaves and halve each artichoke lengthwise; set aside.
6. Place artichoke halves on rack or in steamer basket, cover pan, and steam 25 to 40 minutes, depending on size of artichokes, or until a leaf near center pulls out easily.
7. Line platter with double thickness of paper towels.
8. Using tongs, transfer artichoke halves to paper-towel-lined platter and place cut-side down to drain.
9. Remove choke from each artichoke half and discard.
10. Divide artichoke halves among 4 plates, top each half with a dollop of mayonnaise, and serve with remaining mayonnaise on the side, if desired.

Chicken-Vegetable Soup

Medium-size yellow onion
Large clove garlic
2 large carrots
Small bunch celery
1 tablespoon vegetable oil
1-pound whole chicken breast, with skin and bones
3 cups homemade chicken stock, or two 13¾-ounce cans
¼ pound mushrooms
6 ounces asparagus spears

Medium-size leek
6 ounces bok choy, or ½ pound spinach
½ cup dry white wine
Salt and freshly ground pepper

1. Halve and peel onion. Chop enough to measure 1 cup.
2. Peel and mince garlic.
3. Peel and trim carrots. Dice enough to measure 2 cups.
4. Wash and dry 2 stalks celery. Chop enough celery to measure 1 cup; set aside. Reserve remainder for another use.
5. In large heavy-gauge saucepan, heat oil over medium-high heat until hot. Add onion, garlic, 1 cup carrots, and celery, and sauté, stirring occasionally, 3 to 4 minutes, or until tender.
6. Meanwhile, rinse and dry chicken breast.
7. Add chicken stock, chicken breast, and 3 cups water if using homemade stock, or 2 cups water if using canned, to saucepan, and bring to a boil over medium-high heat.
8. Cover pan, reduce heat to low, and simmer 20 minutes.
9. Wipe mushrooms clean with damp paper towels and trim stems. Cut into ¼-inch-thick slices; set aside.
10. Rinse and dry asparagus. Bend spears to snap off tough woody portions; discard. Cut spears on diagonal into 1½-inch-long pieces to measure about 1 cup; set aside.
11. Trim leek and split lengthwise. Rinse thoroughly to remove sand and grit. Cut leek crosswise into 1½-inch-wide pieces, then cut each piece lengthwise into very thin slices to measure ½ cup; set aside.
12. If using bok choy, rinse and dry. Cut stalks on diagonal into 1-inch-wide pieces to measure 2 cups; set aside. If using spinach, wash thoroughly and dry. Stack leaves and cut crosswise into 1-inch-wide pieces; set aside.
13. Remove chicken breast from broth and pour broth through large strainer set over large bowl, pressing on solids left in strainer with back of spoon to extrude as much liquid as possible.
14. Return broth to pan, add wine, and bring to a boil over medium-high heat.
15. Reduce heat to medium-low, add mushrooms and remaining carrots, and simmer, uncovered, 10 minutes.
16. Meanwhile, remove skin and bones from chicken and discard. Cut chicken on diagonal into thin strips; set aside.
17. Add chicken, asparagus, leek, and bok choy or spinach to broth and simmer another 5 minutes.
18. Add salt and pepper to taste, divide soup among 4 bowls, and serve.

Strawberries with Lemon and Mint

¼ cup granulated sugar
¼ cup julienned lemon peel
1 tablespoon lemon juice
1 pint strawberries
1 tablespoon chopped fresh mint, or ¼ teaspoon dried

1. In small heavy-gauge nonaluminum saucepan, combine sugar, lemon peel, lemon juice, and ¼ cup water, and bring to a boil, stirring, over medium-high heat; continue boiling 5 minutes.

2. Meanwhile, rinse and dry strawberries. Hull berries, and halve if very large. Place berries in medium-size bowl, cover, and refrigerate until ready to serve.
3. Remove syrup from heat and set aside to cool.
4. Just before serving, pour syrup over chilled berries, add mint, and stir gently to combine. Divide among 4 dessert dishes.

ADDED TOUCH

These moist, dense brownies are delicious served alone or with fruit desserts.

Decadent Brownie Bars

Pastry layer:
1¾ cups all-purpose flour
½ cup granulated sugar
½ teaspoon baking powder
¼ teaspoon salt
1 stick unsalted butter or margarine, at room temperature
1 egg, at room temperature

Brownie layer:
1 stick unsalted butter or margarine
3 tablespoons unsweetened cocoa
1 cup granulated sugar
2 eggs, at room temperature
1 tablespoon dark rum
¾ cup all-purpose flour
¼ teaspoon salt
¾ cup seedless raspberry preserves
¼ cup chopped hazelnuts

1. Preheat oven to 350 degrees.
2. For pastry layer, combine flour, sugar, baking powder, and salt in medium-size bowl and stir with fork to blend.
3. Cut butter into pieces and add to dry ingredients. Cut in butter until mixture resembles small peas.
4. Add egg and stir with fork until well blended.
5. Press mixture into bottom of ungreased 8-inch-square baking pan and bake 20 minutes, or until toothpick inserted in center comes out clean.
6. While pastry layer is baking, prepare brownie layer: Melt butter in small heavy-gauge saucepan over medium-low heat; transfer butter to medium-size bowl.
7. Add cocoa to melted butter and stir until blended.
8. Stir in sugar.
9. Add eggs, one at a time, beating well after each addition until totally incorporated.
10. Add rum, flour, and salt, and stir until well blended; set brownie batter aside.
11. Remove pastry layer from oven; leave oven at 350 degrees. Spread pastry with raspberry preserves, then top with brownie batter and smooth out with flexible-blade spatula. Sprinkle evenly with hazelnuts and bake another 25 to 30 minutes, or until toothpick inserted in center of brownie layer comes out clean.
12. Transfer pan to wire rack and set aside to cool.
13. Cut brownies into bars and serve.

Warren V. Mah

A specialist in Oriental cookery, Warren Mah has selected three traditional Japanese meals for this volume. "My menus show that Japanese cooking is not hard to do," he says, "even though the names of the recipes may sound complicated." All of his dishes are light, and the washing and chopping of the ingredients can be done well in advance of mealtime.

Menu 1 offers *teriyaki*, which translates as "shining broil." A *teriyaki* dish comprises meat, fish, poultry, or vegetables marinated in and then glazed with a soy-based sauce. *Teriyaki* foods may be broiled, boiled, steamed, or sautéed. For this meal, Warren Mah marinates and sautés scallion-filled pork rolls and accompanies them with stir-fried vegetables and bowls of white rice.

For Menu 2, he presents a main course of *sukiyaki* (pronounced *skee-yáh-kee*), which means "broiled on the blade of a plow." (In ancient times, Japanese farmers and hunters often killed wild animals and cooked the meat over an open fire with improvised utensils.) Today, *sukiyaki* is generally cooked at the table in restaurants, but at home it is best prepared in the kitchen for safety's sake. This *sukiyaki* features slices of chicken breast, tofu, noodles, and an assortment of vegetables, and is accompanied by a salad of bean sprouts, lettuce, and carrots tossed with a tart *tofu* dressing.

Menu 3 highlights *tempura*, or foods dipped in batter and then quickly fried. Here, the tempura is composed of shrimp and vegetables, and served with a delicious dipping sauce. A light *miso* and watercress soup introduces the meal.

Food prepared Japanese-style should please the eye as well as the palate: Arrange the pork rolls in a semicircle around the stir-fried vegetables and enoki *mushrooms. A bowl of white rice is the traditional accompaniment.*

Pork and Scallion Rolls with Teriyaki Sauce
Stir-Fried Carrots, Snow Peas, and Enoki Mushrooms
Steamed White Rice

P ork wrapped around scallions and marinated in a sweet gingered *teriyaki* sauce is called *butaniku-no-negimaki* in Japanese. In this recipe, the *teriyaki* sauce is used to flavor and tenderize the meat before cooking and to baste it during sautéing. The marinade is traditionally made with *mirin*—a sweet Japanese rice wine—but here the cook substitutes *sake*, a rice wine that is not as sweet. *Sake* is sold in most liquor stores and Oriental markets. If you prefer, you can barbecue the pork rolls, or substitute beef or chicken for the pork, with equally good results.

The bright vegetable combination includes *enoki* (or *enokitaki*) mushrooms—slender ivory-colored stalks that look like tiny umbrellas. These mushrooms are increasingly available in well-stocked supermarkets, specialty produce stores, and Oriental groceries. Refrigerate them in the original package, or wrapped in paper towels, and use them as soon as possible. Because *enoki* are fragile, cook them just long enough to heat them through. If they are not available, thinly slice ¼ pound large cultivated white mushrooms, and cook them as you would the *enoki*.

Rinsing rice until the water runs clear is a traditional Asian practice: A thorough rinsing not only removes any starchy residue left from milling but also produces cooked rice that is lighter and more tender. Swish the grains gently with your hands, taking care not to break them.

WHAT TO DRINK

Cold beer—especially a Japanese brand—goes well with the pork rolls. For a more exotic flavor, you could also serve warm *sake*.

SHOPPING LIST AND STAPLES

8 boneless pork loin cutlets, trimmed and pounded to ¼- to ⅛-inch thickness (about 1 pound total weight)
2 large carrots (about ½ pound total weight)
¼ pound snow peas
3½-ounce package enoki mushrooms
Large bunch scallions
1½-inch piece fresh ginger
2 tablespoons vegetable oil
½ teaspoon Oriental sesame oil, approximately
½ cup Japanese soy sauce

1 cup long-grain white rice (not converted)
¼ cup sugar, approximately
Salt
Freshly ground white pepper
2 tablespoons sake

UTENSILS

Large heavy-gauge skillet
Large sauté pan or wok
Steamer unit, or heavy-gauge saucepan large enough to accommodate bamboo steamer or other steamer insert with cover
Bamboo steamer or steamer insert (if not using steamer unit)
Small saucepan
Glass or ceramic baking dish
Heatproof platter
2 medium-size heatproof bowls
Small bowl
Strainer
Measuring cups and spoons
Chef's knife
Paring knife
2 wooden spoons
Metal tongs
Vegetable peeler
Kitchen string

START-TO-FINISH STEPS

1. Follow pork rolls recipe steps 1 through 6.
2. Follow rice recipe steps 1 through 3.
3. While rice is steaming, follow vegetables recipe steps 1 through 8.
4. Follow rice recipe step 4.
5. Follow pork rolls recipe steps 7 through 13 and serve with vegetables and rice.

RECIPES

Pork and Scallion Rolls with Teriyaki Sauce

1½-inch piece fresh ginger
½ cup Japanese soy sauce
¼ cup sugar
Large bunch scallions

2 tablespoons sake
8 boneless pork loin cutlets, trimmed
   and pounded to ¼- to ⅛-inch thickness (about 1 pound
   total weight)
1 tablespoon vegetable oil

1. Mince enough ginger to measure 2 tablespoons.
2. For marinade, combine soy sauce, sugar, and ginger in small saucepan and bring to a boil over medium-high heat. Reduce heat and simmer 5 minutes.
3. Meanwhile, rinse scallions under cold running water and dry with paper towels. Trim ends and discard. Halve scallions crosswise; set aside.
4. Remove marinade from heat, add sake, and set aside to cool.
5. Divide scallion halves into 8 equal bunches. Gather one bunch of scallion halves, place at edge of one short end of cutlet, and roll tightly. Using kitchen string, tie pork roll firmly, but not too tightly, in two places. Repeat with remaining cutlets.
6. Place pork rolls in glass or ceramic baking dish, add marinade, and set aside for 30 minutes, turning pork rolls every 10 minutes.
7. Remove pork rolls from dish and pat dry with paper towels. Pour marinade through strainer set over small bowl and reserve.
8. Place 4 dinner plates and platter in preheated 200-degree oven to warm.
9. Heat vegetable oil in large heavy-gauge skillet over medium-high heat until hot. Add pork rolls and sauté about 3 minutes, or until lightly brown on all sides.
10. Lower heat to medium and continue to cook, turning pork occasionally with tongs, 3 to 4 minutes.
11. Add about ¼ cup of reserved marinade to skillet and continue to cook pork, basting with sauce, another 2 to 3 minutes, or until pork is firm to the touch.
12. Transfer pork rolls to warm platter, remove string, and carefully cut each roll on the diagonal into 4 pieces.
13. Divide pork rolls among 4 warm dinner plates, arranging them decoratively around edges of plates. Top each serving with a spoonful of sauce and serve.

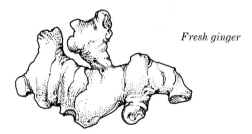

Fresh ginger

Stir-Fried Carrots, Snow Peas, and Enoki Mushrooms

2 large carrots (about ½ pound total weight)
¼ pound snow peas
3½-ounce package enoki mushrooms
1 tablespoon vegetable oil
½ teaspoon Oriental sesame oil, approximately

Pinch of sugar
Salt
Freshly ground white pepper

1. Preheat oven to 200 degrees.
2. Peel and trim carrots. Cut crosswise into 2-inch-long pieces. Halve each piece lengthwise, then cut lengthwise into ¼-inch julienne; set aside.
3. Place snow peas in colander and rinse under cold running water; drain and dry with paper towels. Trim ends and remove strings. Cut snow peas lengthwise into thin strips; set aside.

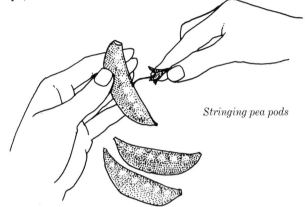

Stringing pea pods

4. Trim root ends of enoki mushrooms and discard; set mushrooms aside.
5. Heat vegetable oil in large sauté pan or wok over medium-high heat. When oil is hot, add carrots and stir fry, adding 1 to 2 tablespoons water to help speed cooking, 2 minutes.
6. Add snow peas and continue stir frying 1 minute.
7. Add mushrooms and stir fry another minute, or just until heated through.
8. Remove pan from heat. Season vegetables with sesame oil, sugar, and salt and pepper to taste. Turn into medium-size heatproof bowl and keep warm in oven until ready to serve.

Steamed White Rice

1 cup long-grain white rice (not converted)

1. Bring 2 cups water to a boil over medium heat in bottom of steamer unit or in saucepan large enough to accommodate bamboo steamer or steamer insert.
2. Meanwhile, place rice in bowl that will fit into steamer or pan when steamer or pan is covered, and add enough cold water to cover rice. With your hands, gently swish rice around until water becomes cloudy. Carefully pour off water, refill bowl with fresh water, and repeat process until water is clear.
3. Drain rice and add enough cold water to cover rice by ½ inch. Place bowl in steamer or pan, cover, and cook rice, without disturbing, 30 minutes.
4. Carefully remove bowl of cooked rice from steamer or pan and fluff rice with fork. Return bowl to steamer or pan and remove from heat. Cover to keep rice warm until ready to serve.

Chicken Sukiyaki
Beansprout, Carrot, and Lettuce Salad
with Tofu Dressing

A major ingredient in this *sukiyaki* is *shirataki* (meaning "white waterfall")—gelatinous, transparent noodles made from a yam-like tuber. Canned *shirataki* are sold in Oriental markets and some supermarkets. If you cannot locate them, substitute bean threads, slender translucent strands made from ground mung beans.

Shirataki need only a brief rinsing, but bean threads require soaking in either hot or boiling water, depending on where they are made: If the bean threads are from

Bring the sukiyaki *to the table steaming hot, and offer chopsticks for dipping the various morsels into individual bowls of raw egg, if desired. The beansprout, carrot, and lettuce salad should be served on separate plates.*

Taiwan or Thailand, use hot water, because boiling water turns them gelatinous. If they are from the People's Republic of China, use boiling water. Do not remove the rubber band before soaking the bean threads, or they will become too unmanageable to cut. When pliable (after about 10 seconds), use scissors to cut through the looped ends or the center of the skein, thereby cutting the bean threads into manageable 4- to 5-inch lengths. Snip the rubber band and discard it, then swish the bean threads in the water to separate them. After another 10 to 15 seconds, when the bean threads are firm, rinse them briefly in cool water and drain again. Now they are ready for use according to recipe directions.

The cook suggests serving individual bowls of very fresh raw egg as an accompaniment to the *sukiyaki*. Tra-

ditionally, the diner beats the egg with chopsticks and then dips the hot food in the beaten egg. The egg cools the food and also seals in the juices.

WHAT TO DRINK

Japanese green tea, warm *sake*, or any type of cold beer would suit this Oriental meal.

SHOPPING LIST AND STAPLES

2 whole boneless, skinless chicken breasts, halved (about 1¼ pounds total weight)
3 blocks firm tofu (each about 10 ounces)
1 pound fresh beansprouts
Small head romaine lettuce
Small bunch watercress
Small bunch scallions
Medium-size onion
Small carrot
1-inch piece fresh ginger
4 very fresh eggs (optional)
½ cup chicken stock, preferably homemade (see page 8), or canned
8-ounce can sliced bamboo shoots

8-ounce can shirataki, or 9-ounce package bean threads
2 tablespoons vegetable oil
2 tablespoons Oriental sesame oil
½ cup Japanese rice vinegar
¼ cup Japanese soy sauce
1-ounce package dried shiitake mushrooms
3-ounce jar sesame seeds
5 tablespoons sugar
Salt
Freshly ground white pepper
2 tablespoons sake

UTENSILS

Food processor or blender
Wok or large sauté pan
Small heavy-gauge skillet or sauté pan
Large saucepan
Large platter
Large salad bowl
2 small bowls
4 small serving bowls or cups (if serving raw eggs)
Salad spinner (optional)
Colander

Large strainer
Measuring cups and spoons
Chef's knife
Paring knife
2 wooden spoons or salad servers
Slotted spoon
Tongs or two 16-inch chopsticks
Vegetable peeler
Grater (if not using processor)

START-TO-FINISH STEPS

1. Follow sukiyaki recipe steps 1 through 11.
2. Follow salad recipe steps 1 through 10.
3. Follow sukiyaki recipe steps 12 through 14 and serve with salad.

RECIPES

Chicken Sukiyaki

1-ounce package dried shiitake mushrooms
2 whole boneless, skinless chicken breasts, halved (about 1¼ pounds total weight)
Medium-size onion
Small bunch scallions
Small bunch watercress
2 blocks firm tofu (each about 10 ounces)
8-ounce can sliced bamboo shoots
8-ounce can shirataki, or 9-ounce package bean threads
1-inch piece fresh ginger
½ cup chicken stock
¼ cup Japanese soy sauce
3 tablespoons sugar
2 tablespoons sake
2 tablespoons vegetable oil
4 very fresh eggs (optional)

1. Place 4 or 5 shiitake mushrooms in small bowl and add hot water to cover; set aside to soften at least 15 minutes.
2. Meanwhile, rinse and dry chicken. Remove and discard any excess fat and tendons. Cut breasts crosswise into ¼-inch-wide slices. Transfer to large platter and set aside.
3. Halve and peel onion. Cutting lengthwise, thinly slice enough onion to measure ½ cup; transfer to platter.
4. Wash and dry scallions. Cut enough scallions into 2-inch pieces to measure ½ cup; transfer to platter.
5. Wash and dry watercress. Trim ends and discard. Transfer watercress to platter.
6. Rinse and dry tofu. Halve, then cut halves crosswise into ½-inch-wide slices; transfer to platter.
7. Turn bamboo shoots into strainer and rinse under cold running water. Drain and transfer to platter.
8. If using shirataki, turn into large strainer and rinse under cold running water; drain. Cut shirataki into thirds; transfer to platter.
9. Rinse and dry mushrooms. Using paring knife, trim stems and discard. Cut caps into ¼-inch-wide slices; transfer to platter.

10. Mince enough ginger to measure 2 tablespoons.
11. Combine chicken stock, soy sauce, sugar, ginger, and sake in small bowl and stir to dissolve sugar; set aside.
12. Heat oil in wok or sauté pan over medium-high heat until a drop of water evaporates on contact. Add chicken and stir fry 2 to 3 minutes, or until it loses its raw look.
13. Move chicken to center of wok or sauté pan and surround it with separate mounds of ingredients from platter. Add stock mixture to pan and bring to a boil. Reduce heat to low and simmer, stirring and turning ingredients without mixing any together, 5 minutes.
14. Bring wok or sauté pan to table and let guests select whatever sukiyaki ingredients they like. Offer bowls of raw egg for dipping the sukiyaki morsels, if desired.

Beansprout, Carrot, and Lettuce Salad with Tofu Dressing

1 tablespoon sesame seeds
1 block firm tofu (about 10 ounces)
2 tablespoons Oriental sesame oil
½ cup Japanese rice vinegar
2 tablespoons sugar
½ teaspoon salt
¼ teaspoon freshly ground white pepper
1 pound fresh beansprouts
Small head romaine lettuce
Small carrot

1. Line plate with double thickness of paper towels. In small dry heavy-gauge skillet or sauté pan, toast sesame seeds over medium-low heat, shaking pan and stirring to prevent scorching, 30 seconds to 1 minute, or until lightly browned. Turn sesame seeds onto paper towels; set aside.
2. Rinse tofu and pat dry. Cut into small chunks.
3. For dressing, combine tofu and sesame oil in food processor or blender and purée.
4. With machine running, drizzle in just enough rice vinegar to make dressing of smooth, pourable consistency. (The amount of vinegar used will vary, depending on water content of tofu.) Add sugar, salt, and pepper, cover container, and refrigerate until ready to serve.
5. Place beansprouts in colander and rinse under cold running water; set aside to drain.
6. Bring 3 quarts water to a boil in large saucepan.
7. Remove and discard any bruised or discolored outer leaves from lettuce. Wash lettuce and dry in salad spinner or with paper towels. Stack leaves and cut enough lettuce crosswise into thin strips to measure 3 to 4 cups; place in large salad bowl.
8. Peel and trim carrot. Using food processor or coarse side of grater, shred carrot; add to lettuce in bowl.
9. Plunge beansprouts into boiling water for 15 seconds, turn into colander, and refresh under cold water. Drain, dry, add to salad bowl, and toss.
10. Turn processor or blender on and off once or twice to recombine dressing. Add 1 cup dressing to salad and toss until evenly coated; reserve remaining dressing for another use. Sprinkle salad with toasted sesame seeds.

Miso and Watercress Soup
Shrimp and Vegetable Tempura

Miso *and watercress soup is the perfect prelude to vegetable and shrimp* tempura, *served with rice vinegar and soy sauce for dipping.*

Properly prepared *tempura* should have a crisp and delicate crust that doesn't coat the food heavily: The color of the food should be visible through the coating. The trick is to make the batter just before it is needed so it does not become thick or gummy. It also helps to have the shrimp and vegetables well chilled, so prepare them in advance and refrigerate them. As the batter-dipped food is lowered into the hot oil, the coating should puff up. For best results, cook the *tempura* quickly, taking care not to overcrowd the food in the hot oil. If the pan is crowded, the temperature of the oil drops and slows the cooking, resulting in soggy food.

The recipes for the soup and the dipping sauce use *katsuo dashi*, a clear stock made from kelp, dried bonito shavings, and other seasonings. Available in an instant dried form in Oriental markets, *katsuo dashi* has a long shelf life. If it is unavailable, you can use half a cup each of hot water and clam juice.

Miso is a seasoning and soup base with a consistency similar to peanut butter produced by fermenting soybeans with rice or wheat. This versatile high-protein paste comes in a variety of colors and is sold in Oriental markets and health food stores. There is no substitute for its unique flavor.

Beer or a crisp white wine, such as a California Sauvignon Blanc or a French Sancerre or Pouilly Fumé, would be good with this menu.

SHOPPING LIST AND STAPLES

1 pound large shrimp
Small bunch watercress
20 snow peas (about ¼ pound total weight)
8 medium-size mushrooms (about ½ pound total weight)
1 Italian eggplant (about 6 ounces)
Medium-size zucchini (about 6 ounces)
2 eggs
8 cups vegetable oil
1 tablespoon Japanese rice vinegar
½ teaspoon Japanese soy sauce
1 tablespoon miso paste
3 cups all-purpose flour, approximately
3 tablespoons cornstarch
2 teaspoons sugar
Two ½-ounce packets katsuo dashi
Salt and freshly ground white pepper

UTENSILS

Wok or large heavy-gauge saucepan
Small saucepan
2 large platters, 1 heatproof
Medium-size bowl
2 small bowls
Salad spinner (optional)
Colander
Measuring cups and spoons
Chef's knife
Paring knife
Wooden spoon
Chinese mesh strainer or slotted spoon
Small whisk
Vegetable brush
Deep-fat thermometer
Small brown paper bag

START-TO-FINISH STEPS

1. Follow tempura recipe steps 1 through 6.

2. Follow soup recipe steps 1 through 6 and serve as first course.
3. Follow tempura recipe steps 7 through 14 and serve.

RECIPES

Miso and Watercress Soup

Small bunch watercress
½-ounce packet (1 tablespoon) katsuo dashi
1 tablespoon miso paste

1. Bring 2 cups water to a boil in small saucepan over medium-high heat.
2. Meanwhile, wash watercress and dry in salad spinner or with paper towels. Trim stem ends and discard. Measure 2 cups loosely packed watercress and set aside; refrigerate remainder for another use.

Watercress

3. Add katsuo dashi to boiling water and return to a boil. Lower heat and simmer gently 2 to 3 minutes.
4. Meanwhile, combine miso paste and ¼ cup of the boiling broth in measuring cup and stir until blended.
5. Add miso mixture to saucepan and return just to the boiling point. Remove pan from heat immediately; further boiling will diminish the flavor of the miso.
6. Divide soup among 4 bowls, add an equal amount of watercress to each bowl, and serve.

Shrimp and Vegetable Tempura

1 pound large shrimp
Salt
Freshly ground white pepper
20 snow peas (about ¼ pound total weight)
1 Italian eggplant (about 6 ounces)
Medium-size zucchini (about 6 ounces)
8 medium-size mushrooms (about ½ pound total weight)
2 eggs

3 tablespoons cornstarch
3 cups all-purpose flour, approximately
8 cups vegetable oil

Dipping sauce:
½-ounce packet (1 tablespoon) katsuo dashi
2 teaspoons sugar
1 tablespoon Japanese rice vinegar
½ teaspoon Japanese soy sauce

1. Pinch off legs of shrimp, several at a time, then bend back and snap off sharp, beaklike piece of shell just above tail, leaving tail intact. Remove shell and discard. Using sharp paring knife, make shallow incision along back of each shrimp, exposing black digestive vein. Extract black vein and discard. Place shrimp in colander and rinse under cold running water; drain and dry with paper towels. Sprinkle shrimp with salt and pepper. Transfer shrimp to small bowl, cover with plastic wrap, and refrigerate.
2. Place snow peas in colander and rinse under cold running water; drain and dry with paper towels. Trim ends and remove strings; place snow peas on platter.
3. Trim and peel eggplant. Halve lengthwise, then cut crosswise into ½-inch-thick slices; place on platter with snow peas.
4. Scrub zucchini with vegetable brush under cold running water; dry with paper towel. Halve zucchini lengthwise, then cut crosswise into ½-inch-thick slices; place on platter with other vegetables.
5. Wipe mushrooms clean with damp paper towels. Trim stems and discard. Place mushrooms on platter with other vegetables, cover platter with plastic wrap, and refrigerate.
6. Preheat oven to 200 degrees.
7. Line large heatproof platter with double thickness of paper towels; set aside.
8. Separate eggs, placing yolks in medium-size bowl and reserving whites for another use.
9. Add 2 cups ice water to egg yolks, and beat with fork until well blended. Add cornstarch and stir until dissolved. Stir in 2 teaspoons salt. Add 1½ to 2 cups flour, a handful at a time, stirring gently with whisk to avoid beating in too much air, until flour is totally incorporated and mixture resembles pancake batter. The batter should have small lumps.
10. Heat oil in wok or large heavy-gauge saucepan over medium-high heat until it registers 375 degrees on deep-fat thermometer.

11. For dipping sauce, combine katsuo dashi, sugar, rice vinegar, soy sauce, and 1 cup hot tap water in small bowl, and stir with fork to dissolve katsuo dashi and sugar.
12. Place 1 cup flour in brown paper bag. If necessary, sprinkle vegetables with water before dredging them to help flour adhere. Place snow peas in bag, close bag, and shake to coat snow peas with flour. Add snow peas to batter. Using Chinese mesh strainer or slotted spoon, remove snow peas from batter, allowing excess batter to drip off. Carefully add snow peas to hot oil and fry, occasionally skimming off any particles of batter that float to surface of oil, 1 to 2 minutes, or until crisp and golden.
13. Using mesh strainer, transfer snow peas to towel-lined platter and keep warm in oven until ready to serve. Repeat process for remaining vegetables and shrimp, adding only as many as fit in pan without crowding.
14. Stir dipping sauce to recombine and divide among 4 small serving bowls. Divide shrimp and vegetables among 4 dinner plates and serve with dipping sauce.

ADDED TOUCH

After a *tempura* dinner, fresh oranges are an ideal dessert because the citrus flavor freshens the mouth.

Gingered Orange Slices

3 navel oranges
½ cup freshly squeezed orange juice
2 tablespoons ginger brandy, or 1 teaspoon crystallized ginger
1 teaspoon cornstarch
2 teaspoons slivered crystallized ginger

1. Using sharp paring knife, peel oranges, removing as much white pith as possible. Cut oranges crosswise into ½-inch-thick slices; set aside.
2. Combine orange juice with ginger brandy or 1 teaspoon crystallized ginger in large sauté pan and bring to a boil over medium heat.
3. Meanwhile, combine cornstarch and 1 tablespoon water in measuring cup, and stir until dissolved.
4. Add cornstarch mixture to pan and simmer, stirring, 1 minute, or until mixture thickens.
5. Add orange slices to pan and cook, turning slices to coat with sauce, 1 minute, or until heated through.
6. Divide orange slices among 4 dessert plates, sprinkle with slivered crystallized ginger, and serve.

Charlotte Turgeon

According to Charlotte Turgeon, "Eating good food with good companions is the essence of happiness." Although she entertains frequently and likes to serve classic gourmet meals, she hates last-minute fuss and bother. By preplanning her menus and precooking some dishes, she is able to spend less time in the kitchen and more time with her guests.

The sautéed chicken breasts of Menu 1 rest on a rich carrot purée and are presented with molded saffron rice and eggplant fans. You can make the purée and the rice in the morning, refrigerate them, and reheat them at serving time.

Menu 2 begins with harlequin canapés: black caviar, chopped egg white, and pimiento on toast rounds. These delicate appetizers prepare the eye and the palate for the beautiful main course of salmon fillets served on a bed of hollandaise-enriched spinach and topped with mousseline sauce (which is simply hollandaise sauce with whipped cream added to it). The basic hollandaise sauce can be made an hour in advance of serving and refrigerated until needed.

Menu 3 is a light and refreshing springtime supper. Cook the asparagus spears and wrap them with the ham, then pour the Mornay sauce over individual portions and refrigerate. You can also prepare the salad ingredients and dressing ahead and refrigerate them separately. Compose the salad just before serving; the ham and asparagus rolls need about 15 minutes to heat.

Candlelight and dark dinnerware create a romantic ambience for this evening party featuring sautéed chicken breasts with carrot purée as the main course. Italian-style eggplant fans and golden saffron rice are the accompaniments.

Sautéed Chicken Breasts with Carrot Purée
Italian-style Eggplant Fans
Molded Saffron Rice

Eggplant fans make a particularly attractive addition to this supper. Select small eggplants that are firm and heavy for their size with clear, glossy skins. Italian eggplants are ideal because they have tiny seeds and tender skins that need not be peeled. For easy slicing, choose elongated rather than squat eggplants. Salting the eggplant slices removes any bitter flavor.

WHAT TO DRINK

A pleasing wine with this menu would be a full-bodied white California Chardonnay or French Burgundy, served lightly chilled.

SHOPPING LIST AND STAPLES

4 small skinless, boneless chicken breasts, halved and pounded to ½-inch thickness (about 1¾ pounds total weight)
4 Italian eggplants (about 1 pound total weight)
8 medium-size carrots (about 1 pound total weight)
Small bunch watercress (optional)
2 shallots
1 clove garlic
1 lemon
2 cups chicken stock, preferably homemade (see page 8), or canned
½ pint heavy cream
6 tablespoons unsalted butter, approximately
¼ cup olive oil
1 cup long-grain white rice
½ teaspoon powdered saffron
½ teaspoon dried thyme
Salt
Freshly ground pepper

UTENSILS

Food processor or blender
Large heavy-gauge skillet
Medium-size skillet
Medium-size nonaluminum saucepan with cover
Small saucepan
2 plates
4 ovenproof 8-ounce ramekins or custard cups
Salad spinner (optional)

Measuring cups and spoons
Chef's knife
Paring knife
Wooden spoon
Wide metal spatula
Metal tongs
Vegetable peeler (optional)

START-TO-FINISH STEPS

At least 2 hours ahead: Follow eggplant recipe steps 1 and 2.

1. Follow rice recipe steps 1 through 3.
2. While rice is baking, follow chicken recipe steps 1 through 10.
3. Follow eggplant recipe steps 3 through 6 and chicken recipe steps 11 through 13.
4. While the chicken sautés, follow eggplant recipe step 7.
5. Follow chicken recipe steps 14 and 15, eggplant recipe step 8, rice recipe step 4, and serve.

RECIPES

Sautéed Chicken Breasts with Carrot Purée

8 medium-size carrots (about 1 pound total weight)
2 shallots
4 tablespoons unsalted butter
1 cup heavy cream
1 lemon
Small bunch watercress for garnish (optional)
4 small skinless, boneless chicken breasts, halved and pounded to ½-inch thickness (about 1¾ pounds total weight)
Salt
Freshly ground pepper

1. Peel and trim carrots. Coarsely chop and set aside.
2. Peel and chop enough shallots to measure 2 tablespoons.
3. In medium-size nonaluminum saucepan, heat 2 tablespoons butter over medium heat. Add shallots and sauté, stirring occasionally, 2 minutes.
4. Add carrots and stir until evenly coated with butter. Cover pan and cook over medium heat, shaking pan occasionally to prevent scorching, 5 to 6 minutes, or until carrots are very tender.

5. Remove pan from heat, uncover, and set carrots aside to cool briefly.

6. Transfer carrots to food processor or blender, and purée. Add cream and process until well blended.

7. Return carrot purée to pan and simmer over low heat, uncovered, 20 to 25 minutes, or until thick.

8. Squeeze enough lemon juice to measure 1 teaspoon; set aside.

9. Wash watercress, if using for garnish, and dry in salad spinner or with paper towels. Set aside 8 sprigs; reserve remainder for another use.

10. Rinse chicken breasts under cold running water and dry with paper towels.

11. Heat remaining 2 tablespoons butter in large skillet over medium-high heat until very hot, being careful not to burn butter. Add chicken breasts and sauté on one side 3 to 4 minutes, or until lightly browned.

12. Meanwhile, place 4 dinner plates under hot running water to warm.

13. Using tongs, turn breasts and brown another 3 to 4 minutes.

14. Dry dinner plates.

15. Add lemon juice and salt and pepper to taste to carrot purée. Divide carrot purée among 4 warm dinner plates, top with chicken breasts, and garnish each serving with 2 sprigs of watercress, if desired.

Italian-style Eggplant Fans

4 Italian eggplants (about 1 pound total weight)
Salt and freshly ground pepper
1 clove garlic
¼ cup olive oil
½ teaspoon dried thyme

1. Wash eggplants and dry with paper towels; do *not* trim stem ends. Remove and discard leaf-like caps from stem ends. Starting ¾ inch below stem end, make three lengthwise cuts through each eggplant.

2. Place eggplants on nonmetal plate and spread slices apart like a fan. Sprinkle cut surfaces of eggplant with salt and pepper, cover them with another plate, and weight plate with heavy can or jar for 2 to 3 hours, or until eggplants are quite limp.

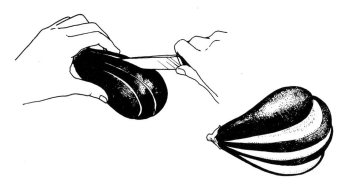

3. Pat eggplant slices dry with paper towels and set aside.

4. Crush garlic under flat blade of chef's knife. Remove and discard peel.

5. Heat olive oil in medium-size skillet over medium-high heat. Add crushed garlic clove and sauté, stirring occasionally, 2 to 3 minutes, or until golden.

6. Remove and discard garlic. Add eggplant fans, sprinkle with thyme, and fry 4 to 5 minutes on one side, or until golden brown.

7. Turn eggplant fans and brown another 4 to 5 minutes.

8. Using wide metal spatula, transfer eggplant fans to dinner plates and serve.

Molded Saffron Rice

2 cups chicken stock
1 cup long-grain white rice
4 teaspoons unsalted butter
½ teaspoon powdered saffron

1. Preheat oven to 350 degrees.

2. Bring chicken stock to a gentle simmer in small saucepan over medium heat.

3. Place ¼ cup uncooked rice in each of 4 ovenproof 8-ounce ramekins. Add ½ cup hot chicken stock, 1 teaspoon butter, and pinch of saffron to each ramekin and stir to combine. Cover ramekins with aluminum foil and bake 30 to 40 minutes, or until rice is tender.

4. Remove rice from oven. Invert each ramekin onto dinner plate, tap with spoon, and remove ramekin to release molded rice. Or serve rice directly from ramekins.

ADDED TOUCH

Fresh strawberries, strawberry jam, and black currant liqueur make a lively filling for these simple tarts.

Strawberry Tarts au Cassis

1 pint fresh strawberries, or 8-ounce package frozen
    unsweetened strawberries, thawed
6-ounce jar strawberry jam
2 tablespoons crème de cassis
½ pint sour cream (optional)
Four 4-inch prebaked tart shells
4 hazelnuts or almonds

1. If using fresh strawberries, gently rinse under cold running water and dry with paper towels. Hull and halve berries; set aside. If using thawed frozen berries, turn into strainer set over medium-size bowl to drain off excess liquid and proceed as for fresh.

2. Heat jam in small saucepan over medium-low heat, stirring, 1 to 2 minutes, or until jam is smooth and spreadable.

3. Remove jam from heat, add two-thirds of berries, and stir to combine. Reserve remaining berries for garnish.

4. Stir in crème de cassis; set mixture aside to cool.

5. If using sour cream, turn into small serving bowl.

6. Divide strawberry mixture among tart shells and smooth tops. Garnish each tart with reserved strawberries, top with a hazelnut or almond, and serve with sour cream on the side, if desired.

Harlequin Canapés
Salmon Fillets and Spinach Hollandaise
with Mousseline Sauce

Harlequin canapés of caviar and egg pique the appetite for salmon with puréed spinach and mousseline sauce.

For the main course, hollandaise sauce is blended with the spinach purée and also forms the base for the mousseline sauce. Despite its awesome reputation, a hollandaise—an emulsion of chilled butter and warmed egg yolks—is not difficult to make, particularly if you follow these guidelines. Take care not to overheat the sauce, so the yolks do not scramble or curdle. The yolks should be whisked until they are as thick as heavy cream, otherwise they will not absorb the butter properly. The butter should be chilled, and each portion thoroughly absorbed by the yolks before you add the next. As soon as all the butter has been absorbed and the sauce has a velvety consistency, remove the pan from the heat to prevent further thickening.

To rescue a slightly curdled hollandaise, stir an ice cube into it, or beat an egg yolk and gradually add the curdled sauce to the yolk, off the heat, until it becomes smooth; then reheat gently.

To fashion the bread rounds for the harlequin canapés, use a biscuit cutter or paring knife and stamp or cut out the rounds as close together as possible to minimize waste. To keep the toasts crisp, do not spread the mayonnaise and toppings on them until just before serving. If you like, you can toast the rounds in advance and keep them in a tightly covered container for up to a week.

WHAT TO DRINK

Choose an acidic white wine, such as a French Sancerre, Pouilly Fumé, estate-bottled Muscadet, or an Italian or California Sauvignon Blanc, for this late-night meal.

SHOPPING LIST

1¼-pound salmon fillet, boned and skinned
Small yellow onion
1 lemon, plus additional lemon (optional)
5 eggs
½ pint heavy cream
1 stick unsalted butter
Two 10-ounce packages frozen chopped spinach
2 tablespoons mayonnaise, approximately
2-ounce jar black caviar
2-ounce jar pimientos
½ loaf sliced home-style white bread (about 10 slices)
1 tablespoon cornstarch
Cayenne pepper
Freshly ground nutmeg
Salt
Freshly ground white pepper

UTENSILS

Food processor or blender
Medium-size nonaluminum saucepan with cover
Small heavy-gauge nonaluminum saucepan with cover
Medium-size baking dish
15 x 10-inch cookie sheet
3 small bowls
Large strainer
Measuring cups and spoons
Chef's knife
Paring knife
Wooden spoon
Wide metal spatula
Rubber spatula
Whisk
Butter knife or spreader
1½-inch biscuit cutter
Nutmeg grater
Electric mixer

START-TO-FINISH STEPS

Thirty minutes ahead: Set out eggs to come to room temperature for canapés and salmon recipes.

1. Follow canapés recipe steps 1 through 7.
2. While eggs are cooling, follow salmon recipe steps 1 through 16.
3. Follow canapés recipe steps 8 through 10 and serve as first course.
4. Follow salmon recipe steps 17 through 22 and serve.

RECIPES

Harlequin Canapés

½ loaf sliced home-style white bread (about 10 slices)
2 eggs, at room temperature
Small yellow onion
2-ounce jar pimientos
2 tablespoons mayonnaise, approximately
Salt and freshly ground white pepper
2-ounce jar black caviar

1. Preheat oven to 350 degrees.
2. Using small biscuit cutter or paring knife, cut out 20 small rounds of bread. Arrange bread rounds in single layer on cookie sheet and toast in oven 8 to 10 minutes, or until lightly browned.
3. Meanwhile, place eggs in small saucepan with enough cold water to cover and bring to a boil over medium-high heat. Reduce heat and simmer gently 8 to 10 minutes.
4. While eggs are simmering, halve and peel onion. Finely mince enough onion to measure 1 teaspoon; reserve remainder for another use.
5. Turn pimientos into strainer and rinse under cold running water; pat dry with paper towels. Cut pimientos into 1½-inch-long by ¼-inch-wide strips; set aside.
6. Remove toasts from oven and set aside.
7. Drain water from eggs and refill pan with cold water to cool eggs. Remove eggs from pan and peel. Rinse eggs under cold running water and dry with paper towel. Place in small bowl, cover with plastic wrap, and refrigerate about 35 minutes.
8. When completely cool, halve eggs. Remove yolks and

place in small bowl; reserve whites. Using fork, crush yolks into a paste. Add minced onion and enough mayonnaise to make the mixture spreadable, and stir with fork to combine. Season to taste with salt and pepper; set aside.

9. Finely chop egg whites; set aside.

10. Spread toasted bread rounds with equal portions of yolk mixture. Holding a very thin knife or an index card at the center of each canapé, cover one side of canapé with caviar and the other side with chopped egg white. Remove knife or card and place a strip of pimiento down center of each canapé. Arrange canapés on platter and serve.

Salmon Fillets and Spinach Hollandaise with Mousseline Sauce

1 stick unsalted butter, well-chilled
1 lemon, plus additional lemon for garnish (optional)
3 eggs, at room temperature
½ cup plus 2 tablespoons heavy cream
Pinch of Cayenne pepper
Salt
Two 10-ounce packages frozen chopped spinach
1 tablespoon cornstarch
Pinch of freshly ground nutmeg
Freshly ground white pepper
1¼-pound salmon fillet, boned and skinned, refrigerated
  until needed

1. Place small bowl and beaters for whipping cream in freezer to chill.

2. Cut butter into 1-tablespoon pieces; set aside.

3. Squeeze enough juice from 1 lemon to measure 3 teaspoons; set aside.

4. To make hollandaise, separate eggs, placing yolks in small heavy-gauge nonaluminum saucepan and reserving whites for another use.

5. Add lemon juice and 3 tablespoons heavy cream to egg yolks and whisk until blended. Cook over low heat, whisking constantly, about 2 minutes, or until mixture starts to thicken.

6. Remove pan from heat and whisk in 2 pieces of butter.

7. Return pan to heat and add 4 more pieces of butter, 1 piece at a time, whisking after each addition until butter is totally incorporated and being careful not to let the hollandaise boil. This operation should take 2 minutes or less. Season the hollandaise with Cayenne pepper and salt to

taste; cover pan and set aside.

8. Preheat oven to 425 degrees.

9. Bring ½ cup of lightly salted water to a boil in medium-size nonaluminum saucepan over high heat. Add spinach to boiling water and return water to a boil while using a fork to break up the frozen spinach blocks. Cover pan, lower heat to medium, and simmer spinach 5 minutes, or just until tender.

10. Lightly butter medium-size baking dish; set aside.

11. Combine cornstarch and 3 tablespoons heavy cream in small bowl; set aside.

12. Turn cooked spinach into large strainer and press with back of spoon to remove as much moisture as possible. Transfer spinach to food processor fitted with steel blade or to blender. Rinse and dry pan.

13. Stir cornstarch mixture to recombine. Add mixture to spinach and purée. Season with nutmeg and salt and pepper to taste.

14. Return spinach mixture to saucepan and cook over medium heat, stirring, 1 to 2 minutes, or just until mixture comes to a boil.

15. Remove pan from heat and set aside to cool to lukewarm.

16. Using rubber spatula, fold two thirds of the hollandaise into spinach mixture. Turn spinach hollandaise into prepared baking dish and cover loosely. Reserve remaining hollandaise.

17. When ready to cook, rinse salmon under cold running water and dry with paper towels. Cut salmon into 4 equal portions.

18. Arrange salmon fillets on top of spinach hollandaise, dot with remaining butter, and sprinkle with salt and pepper to taste. Bake 14 minutes, or until fish flakes easily.

19. Meanwhile, rinse lemon, if using for garnish, and dry with paper towel. Cut crosswise into 8 thin slices and cut notch in each slice to facilitate twisting; set aside.

20. In chilled bowl, beat remaining ¼ cup heavy cream with electric mixer at high speed until stiff.

21. To make mousseline sauce, gently fold whipped cream into remaining hollandaise and warm briefly over medium-low heat.

22. Remove baking dish from oven and, using wide metal spatula, divide salmon and spinach hollandaise among 4 dinner plates. Top with equal portions of mousseline sauce and garnish each serving with 2 slices of lemon, if desired.

Ham and Asparagus Rolls with Mornay Sauce
Avocado and Orange Salad

Serve the ham and asparagus rolls with Mornay sauce in individual gratin dishes, with avocado and orange salad on the side.

A rich Mornay sauce crowns the rolled ham and asparagus. Supposedly named for the French nobleman Philippe de Mornay, who created it, this sauce is simply a basic white sauce enriched by the addition of cheese. For a foolproof Mornay sauce, always cook the butter-flour paste over low heat, and once you have added the milk, simmer the mixture until it is reduced and thickened. Grate the cheese finely so it melts easily into the sauce.

WHAT TO DRINK

A firm and fragrant white wine would be harmonious with this menu. Select a California or Alsatian Gewürztraminer or an Alsatian Riesling.

SHOPPING LIST AND STAPLES

8 thin square slices boiled ham (about ½ pound)
24 asparagus spears (about 1½ pounds total
   weight)
2 medium-size avocados
1 head leaf lettuce
1 clove garlic
2 lemons
1 navel orange, or 11-ounce can mandarin oranges

2 cups milk
4 tablespoons unsalted butter
¼ pound medium-sharp Cheddar cheese
3 tablespoons olive oil
3 tablespoons peanut oil
2-ounce can flat anchovy fillets
Hot pepper sauce
¼ cup all-purpose flour
¼ teaspoon granulated sugar
Paprika
Salt and freshly ground white pepper

UTENSILS

Food processor (optional)
Large skillet with cover
Small nonaluminum saucepan with cover
4 individual gratin dishes or 13 x 9-inch baking dish
Small nonaluminum bowl
Strainer
Measuring cups and spoons
Chef's knife
Paring knife
Whisk
Grater (if not using processor)

START-TO-FINISH STEPS

The night before: If using mandarin oranges for salad recipe, place in refrigerator to chill.

1. Follow ham and asparagus recipe steps 1 through 3.
2. While asparagus is cooking, follow salad recipe steps 1 through 5.
3. Follow ham and asparagus recipe steps 4 through 10.
4. Follow salad recipe steps 6 through 9 and ham and asparagus recipe steps 11 and 12, and serve.

RECIPES

Ham and Asparagus Rolls with Mornay Sauce

24 asparagus spears (about 1½ pounds total weight)
Salt
8 thin square slices boiled ham (about ½ pound)
4 tablespoons unsalted butter
¼ cup all-purpose flour
¼ pound medium-sharp Cheddar cheese
2 cups milk
Freshly ground white pepper
Paprika
2-ounce can flat anchovy fillets

1. Preheat oven to 400 degrees
2. Using paring knife, trim asparagus spears to remove tough, woody ends. Peel stalks and rinse them under cold running water.
3. Place asparagus in large skillet with ½ inch lightly salted cold water and bring water to a boil over medium-

high heat. Cover pan and cook asparagus about 8 minutes, or just until tender.
4. Drain asparagus and refresh under cold running water. Drain and pat dry with paper towels.
5. Roll 3 asparagus spears in each slice of ham and divide rolls among 4 individual gratin dishes, or arrange in single layer in baking dish; set aside.
6. Melt butter in small nonaluminum saucepan over medium-low heat. Whisk in flour, cover pan, and simmer gently over very low heat 2 to 3 minutes.
7. Meanwhile, using food processor fitted with shredding disk, or grater, finely shred enough cheese to measure 1 cup; set aside.
8. Whisking continuously, add milk to butter-flour mixture in a slow, steady stream, and whisk until thick and smooth.
9. Add cheese and continue whisking until cheese melts. Season sauce with salt and pepper to taste.
10. Pour sauce over ham and asparagus rolls, leaving asparagus tips exposed. Sprinkle with paprika and bake 15 to 20 minutes, or until sauce bubbles.
11. Place anchovies in strainer and rinse under cold water; set aside to drain.
12. Remove ham and asparagus rolls from oven and garnish each with 2 anchovy fillets. Serve directly from gratin dishes, if using, or divide among 4 dinner plates.

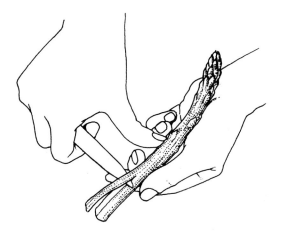

Peel bottom portion of asparagus.

Avocado and Orange Salad

1 head leaf lettuce
2 lemons
2 medium-size avocados
1 clove garlic
3 tablespoons peanut oil
3 tablespoons olive oil
¾ teaspoon salt
¼ teaspoon granulated sugar
Hot pepper sauce
1 navel orange, or 11-ounce can mandarin oranges, well chilled

1. Wash lettuce and dry with paper towels. Stack 6 to 8

leaves and roll them up tightly lengthwise. Cut rolls crosswise into ¼-inch-wide strips. Place strips in plastic bag, close bag, and shake to separate lettuce; refrigerate until ready to use.

2. Squeeze enough lemon juice to measure 6 tablespoons; set aside.

3. Peel avocados and halve crosswise, cutting around pits. Twist halves in opposite directions to separate; remove and discard pits. Place avocados on large plate. To prevent discoloration, coat each avocado half with 1 tablespoon lemon juice. Cover with plastic wrap and refrigerate until ready to use.

4. Peel and mince garlic.

5. Combine garlic, remaining 2 tablespoons lemon juice, oils, salt, sugar, and hot pepper sauce to taste in small nonaluminum bowl and beat with fork until blended; set aside.

6. Peel navel orange, if using, removing as much white pith as possible. Using sharp paring knife, segment orange. Or, if using mandarin oranges, drain and set aside.

7. Line 4 salad plates with lettuce.

8. Remove chilled avocado halves from refrigerator and cut thin slice from bottom of each half so that it will rest flat on lettuce; divide avocados among lettuce-lined plates.

9. Stir dressing to recombine and fill cavity of each avocado half with equal portion of dressing. Arrange orange sections around avocado halves and serve.

ADDED TOUCHES

Tortoni is a popular Italian ice cream with a mousse-like consistency and a macaroon-crumb garnish. In this version, the dessert chills for twelve hours but is not frozen.

Apricot Tortoni

8-ounce package dried apricots
2 tablespoons Grand Marnier, or other orange-flavored liqueur
2 tablespoons blanched slivered almonds
1 egg, at room temperature
2 almond macaroons, or 6 vanilla wafers
1 cup heavy cream
⅓ cup sifted confectioners' sugar
4 mint sprigs for garnish (optional)

1. Preheat oven to 350 degrees.

2. Place medium-size bowl for whipping cream in freezer to chill.

3. Using kitchen shears, snip enough apricots into small pieces to measure ¼ cup. Combine apricots and liqueur in small bowl and stir to combine. Cover bowl and let stand 30 minutes.

4. Spread almonds in single layer on baking sheet and toast in oven, shaking pan occasionally to prevent scorching, about 5 minutes, or until lightly browned.

5. Meanwhile, separate egg, placing white in small non-

aluminum bowl and reserving yolk for another use. Beat white until stiff.

6. Place almond macaroons or vanilla wafers between 2 sheets of waxed paper and crush with rolling pin; set crumbs aside.

7. Remove almonds from oven and set aside to cool.

8. Meanwhile, pour cream into chilled bowl and beat with electric mixer at high speed until cream stands in soft peaks.

9. Gently fold in sugar, almonds, and apricots. Fold in stiffly beaten egg white until totally incorporated and no streaks remain.

10. Divide mixture among 4 sherbet glasses and sprinkle each serving with 1 tablespoon of cookie crumbs. Cover with plastic wrap and chill at least 12 hours.

11. Just before serving, cut 4 apricots into decorative shape for garnish, if desired.

12. Remove desserts from refrigerator and garnish each serving with an apricot and a mint sprig, if desired.

Taramosalata is a rich-tasting yet inexpensive Greek spread made from carp roe. It is sold in jars in specialty food stores or Middle-Eastern groceries.

Taramosalata Tomatoes

4 small tomatoes (about 1 pound total weight)
Small bunch fresh dill
6-ounce jar taramosalata
3 tablespoons mayonnaise
1 head Boston lettuce
2-ounce jar capers
1 loaf French bread or 1 package Melba toast (optional)

1. Wash tomatoes and dry with paper towels. Trim ½-inch-thick slice off top of each tomato and squeeze tomatoes gently to remove seeds. Turn tomatoes upside-down on paper-towel-lined plate, cover with plastic wrap, and place in refrigerator to drain.

2. Rinse and dry dill. Set aside 4 sprigs for garnish and snip enough dill to measure 2 teaspoons. Reserve remainder for another use.

3. In small nonaluminum bowl, combine ½ cup taramosalata, mayonnaise, and freshly snipped dill, and stir with fork to blend. Cover and refrigerate until ready to serve.

4. Wash and dry lettuce. Divide among 4 salad plates; set aside.

5. Turn capers into small strainer and rinse under cold running water; set aside to drain.

6. Place 1 tomato in center of each lettuce-lined plate and fill center of each tomato with equal portion of taramosalata. Spoon capers around outside edge of taramosalata, top each tomato with 1 sprig of dill, and serve with French bread or Melba toast, if desired.

Margaret Fraser

Proud of her Canadian heritage, Margaret Fraser prepares traditional meals as often as possible using indigenous ingredients. The menus she offers here highlight a number of Canadian regional foods in ethnic dishes.

Menus 1 and 3 show the influence of the large Italian populations in Quebec and Ontario. The entrée of Menu 1 is Margaret Fraser's variation on the classic Italian frittata, or open-faced omelet: She bakes the eggs in individual dishes instead of cooking them on top of the stove. Golden caviar pie, a delicacy made with whitefish roe, is the first course.

Menu 3 combines sea scallops (found in abundance in the coastal provinces of British Columbia and Nova Scotia) with Italian *capelli d'angelo* ("angel hair") pasta. As an accompaniment to the pasta dish, the cook serves a simple salad of marinated mushrooms, endive, and romaine lettuce and, after the meal, a special coffee made with Canadian rye whisky and maple-flavored liqueur and topped with heavy cream.

The *tourtière* turnovers of Menu 2 are a quick-cooking adaptation of the traditional French-Canadian pork pie, which is often served in Quebec at *réveillon*, the meal eaten after midnight mass on Christmas Eve. A creamy asparagus soup precedes the turnovers, and for dessert there are wild blueberries with maple cream, another Québecois specialty.

For an informal party, gather friends in the kitchen while you prepare the frittatas and whole-wheat biscuits. While they bake, offer caviar pie with celery sticks for dipping.

Golden Caviar Pie
Individual Frittatas with Leeks and Peaches
Whole-Wheat Biscuits

A frittata is a versatile egg dish that can successfully include a wide variety of flavorful ingredients such as this unusual combination of leeks, red pepper, peaches, and Cheddar cheese. When purchasing leeks, select those that are straight and slender; bulbous leeks are often woody and flavorless. Be sure to rinse leeks thoroughly to get rid of any sand trapped between the layers. If peaches are not in season, use nectarines, apricots, or plums.

The frittatas can be served hot or at room temperature and can be prepared in advance. If they are to be served hot, follow recipe steps 1 through 13 and refrigerate the frittatas unbaked; then bake them just before serving. If they are to be served at room temperature, bake ahead and let cool.

WHAT TO DRINK

To accompany the caviar dish and the frittatas, serve a white wine with finesse: a California Pinot Blanc, an Italian Pinot Bianco, or an Alsatian Sylvaner.

SHOPPING LIST AND STAPLES

Small bunch celery
Medium-size red bell pepper
Small bunch scallions
2 medium-size leeks
1 bunch parsley
2 peaches (about ½ pound total weight), plus
    1 small peach for garnish (optional)
4 large eggs
¾ cup milk
8-ounce container sour cream
4 tablespoons unsalted butter
¼ pound Cheddar cheese
3 tablespoons plus 1 teaspoon shortening
1¾-ounce jar golden whitefish caviar
2-ounce jar black or red caviar for garnish (optional)
¼ teaspoon hot pepper sauce
2 slices firm home-style white bread
1 cup all-purpose flour
1 cup whole-wheat flour
1 tablespoon double-acting baking powder
1 packet unflavored gelatin
½ teaspoon dry mustard
Salt and freshly ground white pepper
2 tablespoons dry white wine or chicken stock
    (optional)

UTENSILS

Food processor or blender
Medium-size skillet
Double boiler
Small saucepan
15 x 10-inch cookie sheet
Four 8-ounce individual baking dishes
Large bowl
Medium-size bowl
Small bowl
Colander
Measuring cups and spoons
Chef's knife
Paring knife
Wooden spoon
Rubber spatula
Whisk
Pie server
2-inch biscuit cutter
Pastry blender or 2 knives
Rolling pin (optional)
Grater (if not using processor)

START-TO-FINISH STEPS

Thirty minutes ahead: Set out eggs to come to room temperature for frittatas recipe.

1. Follow caviar pie recipe steps 1 through 7.
2. Follow biscuits recipe steps 1 through 7.
3. While biscuits are baking, follow frittatas recipe steps 1 through 13.
4. Follow biscuits recipe step 8 and frittatas recipe step 14.
5. While frittatas are baking, follow caviar pie recipe step 8 and serve as first course.
6. Follow frittatas recipe steps 15 and 16 and biscuits recipe step 9.
7. Follow frittatas recipe step 17, biscuits recipe step 10, and serve.

RECIPES

Golden Caviar Pie

1 teaspoon unflavored gelatin
2 tablespoons dry white wine, chicken stock, or water
2 scallions

1 cup sour cream
½ teaspoon dry mustard
1¾-ounce jar golden whitefish caviar
Small bunch celery
2-ounce jar black or red caviar for garnish (optional)

1. Bring 2 cups water to a boil in bottom of double boiler over medium heat.
2. Meanwhile, combine gelatin and wine, stock, or water in top of double boiler.
3. Reduce heat to a simmer, place gelatin mixture *over*, not in, simmering water, and heat, stirring, until gelatin is completely dissolved. Remove double boiler from heat.
4. Wash scallions under cold running water and dry with paper towel. Trim ends and discard. Chop enough scallions to measure ¼ cup.
5. In medium-size bowl, combine sour cream, scallions, dry mustard, and golden caviar, and stir until blended.
6. Fold in dissolved gelatin. Turn mixture into glass pie plate or shallow serving dish and smooth top with rubber spatula. Cover with plastic wrap; refrigerate until ready to serve.
7. Separate celery stalks and rinse under cold running water; dry with paper towels. Trim root ends, and leaf ends if desired, and discard. Cut each stalk crosswise, then halve each piece lengthwise. Wrap celery sticks in plastic and refrigerate until ready to serve.
8. When ready to serve, remove caviar pie and celery sticks from refrigerator. Spoon black or red caviar in decorative pattern over pie, if desired, and serve with celery sticks.

Individual Frittatas with Leeks and Peaches

2 medium-size leeks
2 peaches (about ½ pound total weight), plus
   1 small peach for garnish (optional)
Medium-size red bell pepper
1 bunch parsley
¼ pound Cheddar cheese
2 tablespoons unsalted butter
2 slices firm home-style white bread
4 large eggs, at room temperature
¼ teaspoon hot pepper sauce
Salt and freshly ground white pepper

1. Butter four 8-ounce individual baking dishes; set aside.
2. Bring 1 quart water to a boil in small saucepan over high heat.
3. Meanwhile, trim roots and all but 2 to 3 inches of green from leeks, split lengthwise, and wash thoroughly under cold running water to remove sand and grit; dry with paper towels. Cut enough leeks crosswise into ¼-inch-wide pieces to measure 1 cup; set aside.
4. Plunge 2 peaches into boiling water for 1 minute to loosen skins, turn into colander, and refresh under cold water. Set aside to drain.
5. Wash and dry pepper. Core, halve, and seed pepper. Cut pepper lengthwise into ¼-inch-wide strips; set aside.

6. Wash parsley and dry with paper towel. Set aside 4 sprigs for garnish and chop enough parsley to measure ¼ cup. Reserve remainder for another use.
7. Remove skin from 2 peaches and discard. Halve peaches, cutting around and under pit to separate halves. Cut peaches lengthwise into ¼-inch-thick slices.
8. Using food processor fitted with shredding disk, or grater, shred cheese; set aside.
9. Melt butter in medium-size skillet over medium heat. Add leeks and sauté, stirring occasionally, 3 to 4 minutes, or until tender but not brown.
10. Meanwhile, trim crusts from bread and tear bread into bite-size pieces. Using food processor fitted with steel blade, or blender, process enough bread to measure ⅓ cup crumbs. Transfer crumbs to small bowl; set aside.
11. Add red bell pepper to leeks, reduce heat, and cook gently, stirring occasionally, 3 minutes.
12. Stir in parsley, remove pan from heat, and set aside.
13. In medium-size mixing bowl, whisk eggs until frothy. Add bread crumbs, hot pepper sauce, and salt and pepper to taste. Gently fold in sautéed vegetables, sliced peaches, and cheese, and pour mixture into prepared dishes.
14. Bake frittatas in preheated 350-degree oven 15 minutes, or until firm and golden.
15. Remove frittatas from oven and let stand 5 minutes.
16. Meanwhile, if using peach for garnish, cut into eight slices.
17. Just before serving, garnish each frittata with a sprig of parsley, and 2 peach slices if desired.

Whole-Wheat Biscuits

1 cup all-purpose flour
1 cup whole-wheat flour
1 tablespoon double-acting baking powder
½ teaspoon salt
⅓ cup shortening (including 2 tablespoons butter)
¾ cup milk

1. Preheat oven to 425 degrees.
2. Lightly grease 15 x 10-inch cookie sheet; set aside.
3. Combine flours, baking powder, and salt in large bowl and stir with fork to combine.
4. Using pastry blender or 2 knives, cut in shortening until mixture resembles coarse crumbs.
5. Gradually add milk, stirring with fork, until mixture forms soft but not sticky dough.
6. Turn dough out onto lightly floured surface and knead lightly 10 times. Pat or roll out dough to ¾-inch thickness and cut out biscuits with 2-inch floured biscuit cutter, placing biscuits on prepared baking sheet. You should have about 10 biscuits.
7. Bake biscuits 15 to 20 minutes, or until lightly browned.
8. Remove biscuits from oven, wrap in foil, and keep warm on top of stove. Reduce oven temperature to 350 degrees.
9. A few minutes before serving, return biscuits to oven and reheat briefly.
10. Turn biscuits into napkin-lined bowl or basket and serve.

Asparagus Soup
Tourtière Turnovers
Wild Blueberries with Maple Cream

I n an authentic French-Canadian *tourtière*, a double crust of homemade pastry encloses a pork filling. These simple *tourtière* turnovers include the same basic filling ingredients as the original dish but are made with frozen puff pastry for convenience.

WHAT TO DRINK

Cold beer goes well with this meal. Or serve a simple red wine such as a young California Zinfandel.

SHOPPING LIST AND STAPLES

½ pound lean ground pork
¾ pound fresh asparagus, or 10-ounce package frozen
2 medium-size leeks
Small onion
Small potato
1 clove garlic
1 pint blueberries, preferably wild
2 cups chicken stock, preferably homemade (see page 8), or canned
1 egg
1 pint half-and-half
½ pint heavy cream
8-ounce container sour cream
3 tablespoons unsalted butter
1-pound package frozen puff pastry
12-ounce bottle chili sauce
2 tablespoons pure maple syrup
¼ cup all-purpose flour, approximately
¼ teaspoon celery seed
¼ teaspoon dried sage
Pinch of ground cloves
Freshly grated nutmeg
Salt and freshly ground white and black pepper

UTENSILS

Blender or food processor
Large nonstick skillet
Medium-size nonaluminum saucepan with cover
Jelly-roll pan
Medium-size bowl
2 small bowls
Colander
Measuring cups and spoons
Chef's knife

The creamy asparagus soup sprinkled with grated nutmeg may be served hot or cold, before or with the entrée of pork-stuffed turnovers with chili sauce. For dessert, blueberries are topped with maple cream.

Paring knife
Wooden spoon
Wide metal spatula
Rubber spatula
Whisk
Pastry brush
Rolling pin
Grater (if not using processor)
Electric mixer

START-TO-FINISH STEPS

One hour ahead: Set out ½ pound puff pastry for turnovers recipe, and frozen asparagus, if using for soup recipe, to thaw.

1. Follow blueberries recipe steps 1 through 4.
2. Follow turnovers recipe steps 1 through 6.
3. Follow soup recipe steps 1 through 3.
4. While leeks are cooking, follow turnovers recipe steps 7 and 8.
5. Follow soup recipe step 4.
6. Follow turnovers recipe steps 9 and 10.
7. While turnovers are baking, follow soup recipe step 5.
8. Follow turnovers recipe step 11 and soup recipe steps 6 through 8.
9. Follow turnovers recipe step 12, soup recipe step 9, and serve.
10. Follow blueberries recipe step 5 and serve for dessert.

RECIPES

Asparagus Soup

2 medium-size leeks
¾ pound fresh asparagus, or 10-ounce package frozen asparagus spears, thawed
3 tablespoons unsalted butter
2 cups chicken stock
½ teaspoon salt
¼ teaspoon freshly ground white pepper
1 cup half-and-half
Freshly grated nutmeg

1. Trim leeks and split lengthwise. Rinse, dry, and cut enough leeks into ¼-inch-wide pieces to measure 1 cup.
2. Wash, dry, and trim fresh asparagus, if using. Cut fresh or frozen asparagus into 2-inch lengths.
3. Melt butter in medium-size nonaluminum saucepan over medium-low heat. Add leeks, cover pan, and cook 5 minutes, or until wilted. Do *not* brown.
4. Add asparagus and toss to combine. Stir in stock, salt, and pepper, and simmer, covered, over medium heat, 10 minutes, or until asparagus is tender.
5. Remove pan from heat, uncover, and set aside to cool.
6. Transfer soup to blender, or in batches to food processor, and purée.
7. Return soup to pan and reheat briefly over medium-low heat.
8. Whisk in half-and-half; heat, but do *not* let soup boil.

9. Divide soup among 4 individual bowls, sprinkle with nutmeg, and serve.

Tourtière Turnovers

Small onion
1 clove garlic
Small potato
½ pound lean ground pork
1 teaspoon salt
¼ teaspoon celery seed
¼ teaspoon dried sage
Pinch of ground cloves
Freshly ground black pepper
1 egg yolk
¼ cup all-purpose flour, approximately
½ pound frozen puff pastry, thawed
12-ounce bottle chili sauce

1. Halve, peel, and quarter onion; set aside.
2. Bruise garlic; remove peel and discard.
3. With food processor or chef's knife, chop onion and garlic.
4. Peel and grate potato.
5. Combine pork, onion, garlic, and potato in large nonstick skillet over medium-high heat; cook 10 minutes, or until pork loses its pink color and potato loses its raw look.
6. Remove pan from heat and stir in salt, celery seed, sage, cloves, and pepper to taste; set aside to cool.
7. Preheat oven to 450 degrees.
8. In small bowl, combine 2 teaspoons water and yolk, and beat with fork just until blended; set aside.
9. On floured surface, roll pastry into 12-inch square; cut into 4 equal squares. Spoon one fourth of pork mixture onto one triangular half of each square, leaving a narrow border. Fold other half over and crimp edges with fork.
10. Place turnovers on ungreased jelly-roll pan and brush each turnover with egg wash. Cut small slits in top of pastry to allow steam to escape and bake 5 minutes.
11. Reduce heat to 375 degrees and bake another 15 minutes, or until turnovers are golden and puffed.
12. Transfer turnovers to 4 dinner plates and serve with chili sauce on the side.

Wild Blueberries with Maple Cream

1 pint blueberries, preferably wild
½ cup heavy cream
2 tablespoons pure maple syrup
½ cup sour cream

1. Place bowl and beaters for whipping cream in freezer.
2. Rinse berries in colander and dry. Place berries in small bowl, cover, and refrigerate until ready to serve.
3. Pour cream into chilled bowl and beat with electric mixer at high speed until soft peaks form. As peaks form, drizzle in maple syrup and continue beating until stiff.
4. Gently fold sour cream into maple cream. Cover bowl and refrigerate until ready to serve.
5. Just before serving, divide berries among 4 small bowls or goblets and top each serving with maple cream.

Capelli d'Angelo with Scallops and Fresh Herbs
Mushroom, Endive, and Romaine Salad
Canadian Coffee Royale

Capelli d'angelo *with scallops, accompanied by a mixed salad, makes a fine late meal. Canadian coffee royale is the finale.*

For an impressive supper that looks complicated but is not, serve *capelli d'angelo* pasta with sea scallops and fresh herbs. Sea scallops cook quickly; take care not to overcook them or they will toughen. Once the pasta is *al dente*, toss it quickly—but thoroughly—with the sauce and scallops. The longer the dish stands before serving, the heavier it seems to become. You can, however, make the sauce in advance and finish the recipe just before dinner.

The Canadian coffee royale is especially delicious garnished with maple sugar. Look for this sugar in block or granulated form in specialty food stores. Brown sugar can be substituted. If your party runs late into the night, you may want to use decaffeinated coffee.

WHAT TO DRINK

Select a white wine that will not overpower the subtle flavors of the herbed scallops and pasta. A dry Chenin Blanc or an Italian Soave would be good.

SHOPPING LIST AND STAPLES

½ pound sea scallops
½ pound button mushrooms
2 small heads Belgian endive
Small head romaine lettuce
Small zucchini
Small red bell pepper
Large clove garlic
Small bunch each fresh basil, chives, and oregano
1 lemon
1 pint half-and-half
½ pint heavy cream
2 tablespoons plus 1 teaspoon unsalted butter
2 ounces Parmesan cheese
½ cup olive oil, approximately
3 tablespoons white wine vinegar
½ pound capelli d'angelo or other thin pasta
Ground coffee for 3 cups strong black coffee
8-ounce jar maple sugar or 1-pound package light brown sugar (optional)
2-ounce jar pine nuts
1 teaspoon fennel seeds
Salt and freshly ground pepper
½ cup Canadian rye whisky
½ cup plus 2 tablespoons maple- or coffee-flavored liqueur

UTENSILS

Food processor (optional)
Large skillet
Small heavy-gauge skillet
Large saucepan
2 medium-size nonaluminum bowls
Small bowl
Colander
Measuring cups and spoons
Chef's knife
Paring knife
2 wooden spoons
Slotted spoon
Cheese grater (if not using processor)
Electric mixer or whisk
Coffee maker

START-TO-FINISH STEPS

1. Follow salad recipe steps 1 through 5.
2. Follow pasta recipe steps 1 through 12.
3. Follow coffee recipe step 1.
4. Follow salad recipe step 6, pasta recipe steps 13 through 16, and serve pasta and salad.
5. Follow coffee recipe steps 2 through 6 and serve for dessert.

RECIPES

Capelli d'Angelo with Scallops and Fresh Herbs

Small bunch each fresh basil, chives, and oregano
Small red bell pepper
Small zucchini
2 ounces Parmesan cheese
Large clove garlic
Salt
½ pound sea scallops
1 lemon
2 tablespoons plus 1 teaspoon unsalted butter
2 tablespoons olive oil
½ pound capelli d'angelo or other thin pasta
½ cup half-and-half
Freshly ground pepper

1. Wash, dry, and mince enough herbs to measure 2 tablespoons each.
2. Wash and dry bell pepper. Halve, core, and seed pepper. Cut lengthwise into ¼-inch-wide strips; set aside.
3. Wash and dry zucchini. Trim ends and discard. Cut zucchini into ¼-inch-wide matchsticks; set aside.
4. Using food processor fitted with steel blade, or grater, grate enough Parmesan cheese to measure about ½ cup. Turn cheese into small serving bowl.
5. Peel and mince enough garlic to measure 1 tablespoon.
6. In large saucepan, bring 2 quarts water and 1 teaspoon salt to a boil over medium-high heat.
7. Meanwhile, place scallops in colander and rinse under cold running water; set aside to drain.
8. Squeeze enough lemon juice to measure 2 tablespoons.
9. Butter waxed paper to cover medium-size bowl.
10. Dry scallops. Halve each scallop into 2 thin rounds.
11. Combine oil and 2 tablespoons butter in large skillet over medium-high heat. Add garlic and scallops and stir fry about 3 minutes, or until scallops are opaque.
12. With slotted spoon, transfer scallops to medium-size

nonaluminum bowl. Sprinkle with lemon juice, cover tightly with buttered waxed paper, and keep warm on top of stove. Reserve oil and butter in skillet.

13. Stir pasta into boiling salted water and cook 5 to 6 minutes, according to package directions, or until *al dente*.

14. Meanwhile, return skillet to medium heat. When hot, add half-and-half, herbs, ½ teaspoon salt, and pepper to taste. Bring to a boil and simmer gently about 3 minutes, or until sauce thickens.

15. Stir in zucchini and bell pepper, and return sauce to a boil. Remove skillet from heat. Taste and adjust seasonings; set aside.

16. Drain pasta in colander. Return to saucepan, add sauce and scallops, and toss gently to combine. Divide among 4 dinner plates and serve with Parmesan on the side.

Mushroom, Endive, and Romaine Salad

Small head romaine lettuce
2 small heads Belgian endive
1 teaspoon fennel seeds
½ pound button mushrooms
⅓ cup olive oil
3 tablespoons white wine vinegar
½ teaspoon salt
Freshly ground pepper
2 tablespoons pine nuts

1. Wash and dry romaine. Tear into large pieces and set aside.

2. Wash and dry endive; separate leaves. Wrap endive and romaine in paper towels and refrigerate. Crush fennel seeds under flat blade of chef's knife.

3. Wipe mushrooms with damp paper towels; set aside.

4. For marinade, combine oil, vinegar, crushed fennel seeds, salt, and pepper to taste in medium-size non-aluminum bowl and beat with fork until blended. Add mushrooms and toss until evenly coated. Cover with plastic wrap and refrigerate until ready to serve.

5. In small dry heavy-gauge skillet, toast pine nuts over medium heat, shaking skillet to prevent scorching, 4 to 5 minutes, or until lightly browned. Transfer pine nuts to small bowl and set aside.

6. Just before serving, line 4 salad bowls with romaine and endive leaves. Using slotted spoon, divide mushrooms among bowls, drizzle with remaining marinade, and sprinkle each serving with pine nuts.

Canadian Coffee Royale

Ground coffee for 3 cups strong black coffee
½ cup heavy cream
½ cup Canadian rye whisky
½ cup plus 2 tablespoons maple- or coffee-flavored liqueur
1 to 2 teaspoons maple or light brown sugar (optional)

1. Place small bowl and beaters for whipping cream in freezer to chill.

2. Using your favorite method, brew coffee.

3. While coffee is brewing, pour cream into chilled bowl and beat with electric mixer until stiff; set aside.

4. Pour ¾ cup hot coffee into each of 4 mugs or Irish-coffee-type glasses.

5. Add 2 tablespoons whisky and 2 tablespoons maple- or coffee-flavored liqueur to each cup and stir.

6. Top each serving with whipped cream, drizzle with remaining liqueur, and sprinkle with grated maple sugar or light brown sugar, if desired. Serve immediately.

ADDED TOUCH

These tiny butter tarts resemble pecan pie in texture and taste, but they do not include nuts. The filling of butter, syrup, egg, and currants should be slightly runny when a knife is inserted, even though the top appears dry.

Butter Tarts

Sweet Pastry for 12 miniature tart shells (see following recipe)

Filling:
⅓ cup currants or dark raisins
2 eggs, at room temperature
¼ cup melted butter
⅓ cup firmly packed light brown sugar
¾ cup corn syrup, preferably dark
½ teaspoon vanilla extract
1 teaspoon freshly squeezed lemon juice

1. Preheat oven to 375 degrees.

2. On lightly floured surface, roll sweet pastry dough out to ⅛-inch thickness. Cut out 12 rounds and carefully fit into miniature tart pans; set aside.

3. Place currants in small bowl, add boiling water to cover, and set aside to plump.

4. Break eggs into medium-size nonaluminum bowl and beat with fork just until combined.

5. Add melted butter, sugar, syrup, vanilla, and lemon juice, and stir just until blended. (Do *not* beat mixture.)

6. Drain currants and add to filling mixture; stir to combine.

7. Fill tart shells two-thirds full and bake 15 to 20 minutes, or until pastry is browned and tops of tarts look dry.

Sweet Pastry

¼ cup unsalted butter, chilled
3 tablespoons vegetable shortening, chilled
1½ cups all-purpose flour
1 egg
¼ cup confectioners' sugar

1. Cut butter and shortening into 1-tablespoon pieces.

2. Combine all ingredients in bowl of food processor fitted with steel blade and process 10 seconds, or just until dough starts to gather around blade.

3. Remove dough and flatten to 1-inch thickness. Wrap in plastic and refrigerate for at least 1 hour.

Acknowledgments

The Editors would like to thank the following for their courtesy in lending items for photography: *Cover:* tablecloth—China Seas, Inc.; silverware—Buccellati, Inc.; plate—Ceramic designer Claire Des Becker. *Frontispiece:* glasses—Baccarat, Inc.; Champagne cooler, candelabra—Christofle; silverware—Ercuis; dishes—Ceralene China. *Pages 16–17:* sushi boards and basket, rice bowls—Japan Interiors Gallery; tablecloth—China Seas, Inc. *Page 20:* tablecloth—Pierre Deux; plates, glass, napkin, tray—Wolfman-Gold & Good Co. *Page 23:* flatware—L. L. Bean; Chinese checkers—Linda Campbell Franklin Collection; mat—Susskind Collection. *Pages 28–29:* flatware—Gorham; plate—Ceramic designer Claire Des Becker; table—Della Fera Collection; napkin—Frank McIntosh at Henri Bendel; tart dish—Louis Lourioux. *Pages 30–31:* plates—Frank McIntosh at Henri Bendel; glasses—Gorham; tart pan—Wolfman-Gold & Good Co.; flatware—Christofle. *Page 33:* flatware—Wallace Silversmiths; napkin—Susskind Collection; tablecloth—Conran's; square plate—Julien Mousa-Oghli. *Pages 36–37:* tablecloth—Linda Campbell Franklin Collection. *Page 40:* stove—Tappan; trivet, salt and pepper mills, platter—Pottery Barn. *Page 42:* plates—Dan Bleier. *Pages 44–45:* black and white platters—Dorothy Hafner; serving fork—The Lauffer Co. *Page 48:* flatware—Gorham; tabletop—Formica® Brand Laminate by Formica Corp.; plates, bowls, napkins, vase—Dorothy Hafner. *Page 51:* tablecloth—Pierre Deux; fork—Wallace Silversmiths; glass—Gorham; plates—Ad Hoc Housewares. *Pages 54–55:* plates—Japan Interiors Gallery; tiles—Country Floors Inc.; pizza board, salad bowl—Pottery Barn; napkins—Leacock & Co.; flatware—Gorham; glasses, mussels bowl—Conran's. *Page 58:* napkin, mat, plate, sauce container—Ad Hoc Housewares; fork—L. L. Bean. *Page 61:* vase, black plate—Sointu; plate—Ceramic designer Claire Des Becker courtesy of Sointu. *Pages 64–65:* napkin, plates—Ad Hoc Housewares; tablecloth—Saint Remy. *Page 68:* glasses—Pottery Barn; table, ladle—Della Fera Collection; purple napkin—Susskind Collection. *Page 71:* dishes—Pottery Barn. *Pages 74–75:* tiles—Country Floors Inc.; plate—Haviland & Co.; flatware—Gorham; rice bowl—Japan Interiors Gallery. *Pages 78–79:* sake cups, sake pot, small bowls—Japan Interiors Gallery; screen—Four Hands Bindery. *Page 81:* platter, white bowl—Eigen Arts; tabletop—Formica® Brand Laminate by Formica Corp. *Pages 84–85:* plates—Mikasa; glasses—Gorham; flatware—Baccarat, Inc.; candles—Pottery Barn. *Page 88:* plate—Villeroy & Boch; square plate—Julien Mousa-Oghli; flatware—Baccarat, Inc.; napkin—Leacock & Co. *Page 91:* plate—Phillip Mueller; napkin—Susskind Collection. *Pages 94–95:* rack, napkins, salt and pepper shaker, bowl—Pottery Barn; tiles—Nemo Tile; tart pans—Louis Lourioux. *Page 98:* tiles—Nemo Tile; flatware—Hermes by Retroneu; bowls, plates, salt shaker—Beth Forer. *Page 100:* napkin—Susskind Collection.

Illustrations by Ray Skibinski
Production by Giga Communications

Index